The Soul's Porter, or a Treatise on the Fear of God
By William Price

The Soul's Porter, or a Treatise on the Fear of God
By William Price

Edited and updated by C. Matthew McMahon and Therese B. McMahon
Transcribed by Josh Hicks

Published by Puritan Publications
A Ministry of A Puritan's Mind
4101 Coral Tree Circle #214
Coconut Creek, FL 33073
www.puritanshop.com
www.apuritansmind.com
www.puritanpublications.com

This Print Edition, 2012
Electronic Edition, 2012
Manufactured in the United States of America.

ISBN: 978-1-938721-67-0
eISBN: 978-1-938721-66-3

TABLE OF CONTENTS

MEET WILLIAM PRICE

William Price (1597-1646), was a Calvinistic minister of the Gospel and one of the active members of the Westminster Assembly until his death during the assembly meetings. He was one of the *Prices* of Denbighshire, where he matriculated from Christ Church, Oxford, on Oct. 16, 1616, aged 19. He graduated with a B.A. and an M.A. on June 21, 1619, and a B.D. on June 14, 1628. Taking holy orders, he was, on Sept. 26, 1621, elected the first reader in moral philosophy on the foundation of Thomas White. On White's death in April 1624 Price preached his funeral oration, which was included in "Schola Moralis Philosophiæ Oxon." in *Funere Whiti pullata*, (Oxford, 1624). In 1630 Price joined in a protest to the king on technical grounds against the appointment of Bishop Laud as chancellor of Oxford (Cal. *State Papers*, Dom. 1629-31 , p. 241). He was instituted on Feb. 10, 1631 to the rectory of Dolgelly, Merionethshire, where he died in 1646, and was buried in the church. He married Margaret, daughter of Robert Vaughan of Hengwert, the antiquary.

Dr. Price was one of the Assembly of Divines at Westminster. His name is both in the ordinance of the Parliament for calling the Assembly, and also in the list of those divines who met in it. In the ordinance of the Parliament, he is said to be, "Mr. Price of Paul's Church in Covent-Garden." In the title-page of his sermon, in 1646, he is said to be "Pastor of Waltham Abbey, and one of the Assembly of Divines." And we find, that in the year 1646, Mr. Obadiah Sedgwick, became preacher at Paul's, Covent-Garden. Mr. Baillie considers Mr. Price among the ablest divines in the Assembly when speaking of his being against the institution of the ruling elder by divine right (Baillie's *Letters*, vol. i. p. 401). Mr. Price subscribed the above-mentioned proposition, respecting Jesus Christ, as King of the Church.

Mr. Price has published a sermon, which is entitled, "Man's Delinquency attended by Divine Justice, intermixed with Mercy," displayed in a sermon from Ezra 9:6-8 to the House of Lords assembled in Parliament, in the Abbey-church, Westminster, Nov. 25, 1646. This was during one of their fast days, (4to. London, 1646). In that valuable sermon, which is part of this present work, Mr. Price has the following choice sayings: 1) We are ashamed of our glory, and glory in our shame. 2) When the soul-wounded publican dared not look up to heaven, heaven looked down to him.

Speaking of sinning against clear light, he says, "Great knowledge greatens sins; for knowledge is like the unicorn's horn, that does well in a wise and good man's hand, but ill on a beast's head."

The known works of William Price include copies of two works that are extremely rare, and two works that have no known copies associated with them. 1. *The Soul's Porter, or a Treatise on the Fear of God*, 1638; and 2. *Man's Delinquency*, a sermon before the House of Commons, 1646. The following two works are unattainable: 3. *Gods Working and Britain's Wonder*. A sermon on Psa. 118:31, congratulating the most happy establishment of...Charles the II on his throne, *etc.* 4to. London, 1660. 4. A *Sermon* on Isa. 1:21-22 preached on Wednesday in Easter Week, April 13, 1642, before the Lord Mayor, *etc.* 4to. London, 1642.

[ORIGINAL TITLE PAGE]

Ianitor Animae:

THE SOUL'S PORTER

To cast out sin and to
keep out sin

A TREATISE

Of the Fear of God.

WRITTEN

BY WILLIAM PRICE,

Bachelor of Divinity, and
Vicar of *Brigstock* in
Northamptonshire.

"The fear of God is the beginning of wisdom," Pro. 1:7.
"Let us hear the conclusion of all: Fear God," Eccl. 12:13.

"Fear is always present to stop us and to block us along the way,"
AUGUSTINE

Printed by *I.D.* for *John Cowper*,
the holy Lamb at the East end of
St. Paul's Church.
1638.

EPISTLE DEDICATORY

To the right honorable, the Lord William, Earl of Salisbury, Captain and Knight of the noble army; one of his majesty's most honorable privy council, and his most noble patron; together with the most noble Lady,

I prefix your worthy and great names before this plain and unpolished discourse; not that I intend to thrust my pen into any quarrelsome theme that may provoke the fury of the *Dans* (Gen. 49:17) of this world, that serpent-like lie in the paths, to bite the heel of every passenger, between whom and me, I should entreat your honors as a screen, to interpose, to hide me from their rage. For sure, no Christian has so far changed his humanity with a beast, or cast himself so many degrees behind the purblind Gentiles, as professedly to bear arms against a book honored with the title of the *Fear of God*. Neither do I arrogantly dare presume that there is anything in the style or conveyance of the subject in hand that merits an admission into your honors' closets, much less into the cabinet of your more serious thoughts, or that may attract an eye of favor from you. My weekly laboring in God's harvest, forbids pomp in language, and ambition of many quotations.

Next, the advancement of God's glory (which as our ultimate end, ought to regulate, moderate, stint, and bound our actions) the scope that I level at, is the unfeigned expression of my gratitude and service, which your constant countenance, your undeserved bounty, your propitious acceptance of my mean sore past labors, does more than challenge from me, who desires to draw his breath, than he shall study to approve himself.

Your Honors' Chaplain in all humble observance,
William Price

Perlegi librum bunc, cuititulus est, Ianitor Animae, *eunque typis unandari permitto.*
Sa Baker

Ex adibus Londin.
Maij penult. 1637.

CHAPTER 1:

The Introduction

It is a triumph of this theological virtue of the *Fear of God*, that those who have least affinity with it, yet applaud it, and profess it. And it is my happiness, that nothing can commend a grace, that is not with advantage centered in this. If I should here declare the nobility, excellency, and transcendence of the fear of God in itself, and the utility, and absolute indispensable necessity of it in reference to us, I should but forestall and prevent myself. It is sufficient to premise, both to excuse my writing, and to provoke all Christians advisedly, diligently, and thoroughly to read this ensuing discourse; that, though many have brief essays, yet few, or none, have done this royal grace the honor, or right to allot to it a complete full treatise. And that that may invite all eyes and minds here, is this consideration, that when many other graces are peculiarly pertinent to persons, as they are members of a family in the threefold combination therein; between husband and wife, parent and child, master and servant; or as they are members of a corporate entity, ecclesiastical or civil. And when other duties receive specification and restriction from circumstances of time and place, this of the *fear of God*, like a well-limbed picture, casts an eye on all that look on it. It corresponds to all persons, none excluded. It is seasonable at all times, sacred and common; especially when the scourges of God lie on neighboring nations, and threaten us. And these thoughts may justly, in all places, press on us without being guilty of unmannerly instruction.

Now, for the methodical contriving of this discourse, I shall (by Divine assistance) pursue that order that may most aptly answer the subject matter, and may be most facile and applicable to the minds and memories of the readers.

CHAPTER 2

Of the nature and kinds of fear. Fear in general, and the fear of God, in particular.

The first inquiry will be, *what the fear of God is.* Where the nature and kinds both of fear in general, and in particular of the fear of God will opportunely fall in.

Now to penetrate the depth of the question, we must distinguish of fear.

1. As it is a natural affection indifferent in itself, neither morally good, nor evil.

2. As it is a habit or quality inherent in the affection.

If we consider fear as it is a natural affection implanted in the reasonable soul of man, indifferent in itself, neither morally good nor evil, *then:*

For the general nature of it, *it:*

1. Either stands aloof, at some distance from its object, admiring and reverencing it, or:

2. It is averse from its object. For affections are of two sorts, either such as cleave unto, and desire a near union with their object, as faith, love, and hope; or such as turn from, and desire a perpetual separation from their object, as hatred, and some kind of fear.

2. If we look into the subject, where this affection of fear is implanted, it will be found to *reside,*

1. In the sensitive appetite, for there is a rational appetite, and that is the will that usually follows the dictate, the guidance of the understanding. And there is an inferior sensitive appetite, which contains within its verge, the passions, disturbances, or affections, which often run before the understanding and the will, being more rash, precipitant, and headstrong. One of these affections is fear.

2. There is a double faculty in the sensitive appetite, namely, the concupiscible faculty which looks on the object under the notion of good or evil, to which head the affections of love, joy, and grief are referred.

The other is called the irritableness faculty, which looks on the object under the notion of difficulty, to which head are to be reduced, hope, which looks on a task that is good to be hard which will be obtained, and fear that looks on some evil, hard to be avoided. This is the subject where fear dwells.

3. For the object of fear, it *is:*

1. Sometimes something good, which we esteem, and fear to lose.

2. Sometimes it is something that is great and potent, which we fear to offend.

3. Sometimes it is something full of majesty, excellency, and glory, which we fear with a reverential fear, with a fear of observance.

4. Sometimes it is something evil. That is, either that which is evil in itself, in its own nature, or that which seems to us to be evil, or that which may prove pernicious and prejudicial to us.

And the evil which we fear is:

1. Future, to come, we are troubled for those things that may come to pass (Matt. 24:6). If an evil is present, we feel it, we hate it, we grieve under it; if it is to come, we fear it.

2. As to the object of fear, it is the future of evil, so also the proximity and imminence of it. We fear that kind of evil most that hangs over our heads, ready to seize us, that like a breed of dog called a Bull Mastive ready to attack, lies at the door (Gen. 4:7), waiting for it to open, that he might fly in our faces. Therefore to frighten men from envy and malice, Saint James says that the judge stands before the door (Jam. 5:9).

3. The object of fear is as the nearness, so the unavoidability, the irresistibility of evil. Evil, like the travail of a woman, cannot be escaped. "For when they say, "Peace and safety!" then sudden destruction comes upon them, as labor pains upon a pregnant woman. And they shall not escape," (1 Thess. 5:3).

We see what the affection of fear is.

Next, we must consider fear as it is a habit, or quality inherent in the affection. And so fear is either moral or spiritual.

Moral fear is either that virtue that is opposite to audacity by which we fear and shun those things that are contradictory to the principles of moral virtue and rectified reason; or else it is taken for that fear that we call fainthearted cowardice, that is contrary to fortitude or magnanimity. When a man is so timid that – as Solomon speaks of the sluggard – he cries when he is put on any action that "there is a lion in the way," (Prov. 26:13). When a man fears more of the show and shadow of evil than the evil itself, as children fear more the helmet than the man. When a man fears that least which he should fear most, and that most which he should fear least. As our brainless dwellers fear more the loss of reputation, when it may be they never had any, than they fear the loss of their souls. And therefore wise men know such single combatants to be the grossest cowards, because they in such a degree fear a cross word, or the giving of the lie. And cowards are most cruel, for they will be sure to kill if they can, lest their enemy surviving should take vengeance upon them. This is moral fear.

2. What spiritual fear is we shall perceive by two or three profitable distinctions, which reflect one upon another, and contribute mutual light to each other, and which all illustrate the matter in hand.

The first distinction is that spiritual fear is fivefold. 1. The fear of a guilty conscience. 2 The fear of a slave. 3. The fear of a servant. 4. The fear of a son. 5. The fear of a chaste and a loving wife.

There is a spiritual fear proceeding from a self-accusing conscience that is like the fear of a felon, either ready to be apprehended, or standing at the bar before his judge; when a man only fears God as his judge, or as his executioner. And this fear is joined with a hatred of God, and with a secret wish that there were no God to condemn us. And this fear is lively and *graphically* expressed in Holy Scripture. It was in Adam after his defection. He hid himself among the trees of the Garden out of fear (Gen. 3:8). It was in Cain after he had made his brother Able the first martyr, and himself the first murderer. "It shall come to pass," he said, "that every one that findeth me shall slay me," (Gen. 4:14). His guilty fear presented him with troops of men, when there were almost no others besides him in the world, and with a thousand deaths when he could only die once. "The sound of a shaken leaf shall chase the disobedient," (Lev. 26:36). "The wicked flee when no man pursueth," (Prov. 28:1, *cf.* Gen. 20:4). They are a terror to themselves (Jer. 20:4), afraid of their own shadows. This guilty fear, the heathen used to compare to Silyphus his restless rolling of the stone, and to Promethius his vulture, which without intermission, gnawed on his heart.

2. There is a slavish fear, when a man fears God as a galley slave fears him that took him captive, whom he would kill or flee from if he could or dared. When a man counts the commandments of God to be bonds and fetters, which they would fain shake off like those that cried, "Let us break his bonds, and cast away his cords from us," (Psa. 2:3). When a man hates to be reformed, like those the Psalmist speaks of (Psa. 50:17). When a man hates God (and such there are, Psa. 139:21), and yet sometimes subjects to God's command because he would not dare do otherwise, as King Abimelech would have taken to himself Sarah, Abraham's wife, but he dared not because God told him in a dream that if he did, he was "but a dead man," (Gen. 20:3). And Balaam would have gladly cursed the people of God at King Balak's request, but that he did not dare, though Balak would have given him his house full of silver and gold (Num. 24:13). So, the devil himself is God's slave, and in many things obeys God, because he does not dare disobey him. It may be said of them that so fear God, as Cicero said of Antronius , they turn themselves sometimes

to fear, but not to faithfulness.[1] When the fear of punishment alone instigates a man to good, in this he offends, because he would commit that evil which he forbears, if his impiety might be met with impunity. This is that fear which divines use to call *servile fear*, and Saint Basil calls *hostile fear*; the fear of an enemy to God.[2] And in this it differs from the fear of an accusing conscience, because that fear reflects upon an evil already committed: this fear prevents the commission of many sins. The fear of a self-accusing conscience is a slavish fear, but every slavish fear is not the fear of a self-accusing conscience.

There is the fear of a servant, which is different from what they call *servile*, or *slavish fear*. For though every slave is a servant, yet every servant is not a slave. And though the fear of a servant is not so good as the fear of a son, yet it is better than the fear of a slave. The slavish fear is mixed with a hatred of God, but this fear is mixed with some final degree of the love of God. Slavish fear drives a man from God, this fear draws a man to God, as that woman that trembled, yet came to Christ and fell down before him (Mark 5:33). This fear is, when a man—having well-studied the Law of God, and compared his

---

[1] *Antronius conventit se aliquando ad timorera rumquam ad sumtaican.* Or. Pro P. Sylla. *Quam quis timorenpane bona agit, in co ipso pecat, quo secare veliet, so inulte potuisset.* Greg..

[2] *Hic timor peccadi facultatem disterre potest, auferre non potest: & quos suspendit acrimine avidiares reddit ad crimen.* Chrysostom.

heart and life with that perfect rule—sees himself fall infinitely short of it, and on it acknowledges himself liable to all the curses of God due to the disobedient, and utterly disclaims all help or worthiness of help in himself; he stands like a man over a vault of gunpowder, the match being ready to be put to the train, and sees no safety but in God's mercy, and Christ's merits, which yet he is fearful to apply to himself, lest he should have no interest in them. This fear is, though imperfect, yet allowable and necessary. "Ye have not," says Saint Paul, "received the spirit of bondage again to fear," (Rom. 8:15), implying that they had before received the spirit of bondage to fear. This fear we call an *initial fear* and everything must have a beginning. The Law, by stirring up this fear, is a "schoolmaster to lead to Christ," (Gal. 3:24). It is like John the Baptist who prepared "the way of the Lord," (Luke 1:76). Like the needle, which does not sew by itself, yet it leads the way to the thread which sews. The compunction of this fear delivers up the soul to the kindly impression of love. And though this fear of a servant we must pass to the fear of sons, and it is one and the same Spirit of God that works both these fears in us, and the one as a preparative to the other.

4. There is a *filial fear* which, though it is joined with a greater degree of love than is in a servant, yet with a less degree of love than is in a loyal wife.

This childlike *fear*:

1. Stands in awe of God for his excellency and transcendent glory, though it expects no evil from God, but good. It will keep a wary distance and not be over-daringly bold. When God had given Jacob fair promises in his sleep, yet awaking he was afraid, and said, "How dreadful is this place! This is no other than the house of God. This is the gate of heaven," (Gen. 28:16, 17). And this is called "a fearing before," or "in the presence of God," (Eccl. 8:12). As when a man stands before his Prince, his majesty strikes a tremendous awe in him; though otherwise he has no reason to be afraid, his conscience bearing him witness, that he has not any way willingly incurred his Prince's displeasure. This is the fear of *reverence*.

2. As this *filial fear* is *reverential*, so it is *careful*, that God our heavenly Father may no way be displeased by us, not only because that God's displeasure may shower down in punishments on us, but because he is our Father, whom we have a tender care to please, he having deserved the flower of our affection and service. "There is mercy with thee that thou mayest be feared," David says (Psa. 130:4).

5. And lastly, there is the fear of a loving and loyal wife, when a man fears God, as a kind wife fears an indulgent husband. And this I make to differ from *filial fear*, not in kind, but in degree. This *conjugal fear* is matched with an unspeakable melting love, and a constant care that no unkindness happen. A son may express his love, but not in the height as a wife may. And though the wife be without *servile fear*, yet she exceeds the son in a fearful (but loving) care that her husband be not displeased, that affection between them may not grow dull and remiss, that there may be no cause given that may occasion so much as a frown, or a cross word, much less a separation. Saint Augustine sweetly sets this forth in comparing *servile* and *filial fear* of God, with a harlot's and good wives' fear of their husbands. (*Illa timet ne venit illa ne defcedat: Illa ne damces illa ne de serat.*) One fears lest her husband should come home; the other fears lest her husband should depart from her, though for a small time. The one fears lest her husband should chide or strike her, the other fears lest he should forsake her. To which I may add, the one fears lest her husband should be angry with her, the other fears lest he should be angry at all. The one fears her own vexation, the other fears her husband's disquiet. This is the genuine true bred fear of God, which Saint Paul makes a sign of true

repentance, never to be repented of, "What carefulness it wrought in you, yea...what fear?" (2 Cor. 7:11), that is, what care, what fear, that the glory of God may not suffer through you. And so much for the first distinction, in which, under several resemblances I have shadowed out but two fears in effect, the *slavish* and the *filial* fear of God. They obtain several names by reason of their different degrees and extents of their operations.

The second distinction is this, that there is a *forced fear*, and a *voluntary fear* of God.

1. The *forced* fear is the *guilty*, the *slavish* fear. For he that is possessed with it, labors to drive it away; to drown it with drinking, merriment, jovial company, vain discourse, or obscene songs: as the ancient Italians would confound the noise of thunder with the sound of bells.

This was Belshazzar's fear when God sent a hand to write his doom upon the wall before his face. He would have continued in his amusement, but such was not so. For whether he wanted it or not, his "countenance was changed, and his thoughts troubled him, so that the joints of his loins were loosed, and his knees smote one against another," (Dan. 5:5-6). Such was the fear of Felix the Roman Governor when he sent for Paul to speak before him. He was so far from thinking that Paul should terrify him, that he thought to terrify Paul. For when Saint Paul "reasoned of righteousness, temperance, and judgment to come, Felix trembled" (Acts 24:24, 25), and he dismissed Saint Paul that he might rid himself of those fits and qualms of fear.

2. There is a voluntary, free, unconstrained fear of God, and such is the *filial fear*, a fear that is desired and prized by him that fears. It is thirsted after, we "desire to fear thy name," Nehemiah says (Neh. 1:11). It is prayed for, "Unite my heart to fear thy name," David says (Psa. 86:11). It is a fear that a saint dedicates and gives himself to, "Thy servant," David says, "who is devoted to thy fear," (Psa. 119:38). It is a fear that by the fearer is esteemed and valued at a high rate, "The fear of the Lord is his treasure," (Isa. 33:6). This is the second distinction.

The third distinction is *this*:

There is a fourfold fear of God.

1. A fear that flows from the Spirit of God, but is not resident in the heart with the Spirit of God. This is that *initial fear* that paves a path for the spirit of adoption, and for the true *filial* fear. The Spirit works many a common grace in that heart in which itself is not, as it works this fear. As the sun before it rises darts light into that part of the heaven and air where he himself is not, so this fear is from the Spirit, but not with the Spirit.

2. There is a fear where the Spirit of God is, and yet it does not flow from the Spirit. As many things may be done by children, or servants in a house, where the father or master is, and yet they may not be the authors of them. So, a soul that is the mansion of the Holy Spirit of God may harbor in it carnal distrustful fears and cares that the Spirit of God has no hand in. This was David's fear that was joined with a dissidence in God's many promises made unto him to the contrary. "I shall perish...one day by the hand of Saul," David said (1 Sam. 27:1). This fear was with, but not from the Spirit.

3. There is a fear that neither proceeds from, nor is joined with the Spirit of God. Such is that unsanctified slavish fear that turns the affection from God and moves a man to fly from God. It was the fear of those in the Psalmist that "were...in fear, where no fear was," (Psa. 53:3-5), and yet they turned back from God. They were filthy, they devoured God's people, they did not call on God. This fear is neither with, nor from the Spirit.

There is a fear that has the Holy Spirit of God both for its original and also its companion. Like that daylight that is both with and from the sun. This is *filial fear*. The Spirit of God is styled the spirit of this fear because it is both from the Spirit and with the Spirit.

These distinctions being well weighed will cast such beams of light upon the matter in question, that he that runs may read the full comprehension of the nature of the fear of God.

CHAPTER 3

How God, being the chief good, can be feared.

If it is asked, "How can God, being good in himself and good to all, be feared, seeing we usually fear only evil?" It is *answered:*

1. That we may fear God with a fear of honor and regard. "If I be a father," says God, "where is my honor? If I be a master, where is my fear?" (Malachi 1:6). In that text, fear and honor are one in the same.

2. Though God is good, and we cannot fear him as evil, yet we may fear a loss of and separation from our good God. The more good anything is, the more we fear the cutting off our benefits in it. And in this sense are those words of Saint Augustine to be taken. "We fear good in fearing lest we should lose that good we enjoy, or not obtain that good we desire or hope for."

3. We may fear our God, though he is good, because he is a great and just God, who is able to save and to destroy, as St. James speaks (James 4:12). Aristotle says, "Those things are to be feared which have an apparent power to inflict great punishments upon us, and to do us much hurt." (Aristotle, *Reht.* 1.2. c. 5.) And this agrees with that of our Saviour, "Fear him who is able to destroy both body and soul," (Matt. 10:28). All punishment comes from God, but in that respect

punishment is good, because it is a work of justice. So we may fear God, though he is good.

Lastly, we may be fearful of offending God in the ingenuity of our dispositions, because he has been, and is every way so good a God to us. "There is mercy with thee, that thou mayest be feared," David says (Psa. 30:4). And these two duties are joined together, "Fear the Lord," and "consider what great things he hath done for you," (1 Sam. 12:24). We fear God not only for that evil that he may do against us, but also for that good that he has done for us. No, fear of God is a thing so proper that some derive θεός (*theos*), the name of God, from Διὸς (*dios*) which signifies fear.

And why is God said to be "fearful in praise" (Exod. 15:11), because we both fear and praise him for his greatness and goodness? The object both of fear and praises may be the same. And to this sounds that of the Prophet, they "shall fear the Lord and his goodness in the latter days," (Hos. 3:5).

CHAPTER 4

Whether Adam in the state of innocency feared God,

and whether the Angels and Saints in heaven fear God.

Adam had the natural affection of fear in his soul while sinless, though he had no occasion to bring it into action, until after he fell, as he in sinlessness had a power, a faculty in him to be pitiful, if there had been an object on which to have pity. And there is no question, but in his innocent estate, he feared God with the fear of honor, reverence, and observance.

Next, for the angels and saints in heaven, though that place will admit of no fear of punishment; because no evil is possibly incident to the blessed, for the celestial paradise is a mansion of eternal security wherein the enjoyers are not only safe, but sure they are safe (*Et silvi & secure*). But yet it does not derogate from their happiness to say that those in heaven do fear God with a fear of honor and reverence. St. Augustine calls this a *secure fear* (*timor secunus*. Aug.). And Gregory in his *Morals*, speaking of those words in Job, says "the pillars even tremble" and "the powers in heaven stand in awe in the contemplation of God," (Job. 26:11).[3] Which fear he says is not a *penal fear*, but a fear of admiration, ecstasy, astonishment at

---

[3] *Virtutes caelestes on Dei contemplation contremiscunt.* Greg. *Non timor penalis, sed idimtrationis.*

the transcendent immensity of God's glory. And we shall offer no violence to that, Psa. 19:9, "The fear of God endures forever," and that, Jer. 32:39, "I will give them a heart to fear me forever," if we fasten this sense on them.

CHAPTER 5

How the fear of God can stand with the love God, with joy, faith, and hope in God.

It may be questioned next how the fear of God can consist and stand with the love of God, and with joy, faith, and hope in God, since it is said that "perfect love casteth out fear" (1 John 4:18), and fear and joy, fear and faith, and fear and hope seem to be contrary and exclusive against one another. To resolve which doubts, we must *know*:

1. For the love of God that, though nothing is more opposite than sincere love and slavish fear, yet none are more near and dear companions than love and the *filial* fear of God. Nothing is more fearful than his love, and nothing is more loving than his fear. Where there is love, there is a fear of the wronging of the thing loved. Love fulfills the law (Rom. 13:10) says St. Paul, and "to fear God and obey him is the whole duty of man," says Solomon (Eccl. 12:13).

Love is a grace that unites and knits the heart to God, and fear is a uniting grace. "Unite my heart to fear thy name," David says (Psa. 86:11). "I will put my fear into their hearts, and they shall not depart from me," says God (Jer. 32:40). Fear and love keep a man equally close to God, and the same promises are made to love and fear in the Psalms (Psa. 145:18-19).

2. The case is as clear for joy in God. If fear and joy did expel each other, David would never have said, "Rejoice with trembling," (Psa. 2:11), neither would he have joined these two counsels together, fear the Lord and rejoice greatly in his commandments, (Psa. 112:1). He that fears to offend God has most cause of joy. He that fears God is truly joyful, others are but lacking. It is said of the two *Marys* that "they departed with fear and great joy," (Matt. 28:8). So that great joy and fear may stand together.

3. The fear of God is no more an enemy to faith in God. Noah believed that God would bring a universal flood on the world, and yet God save him from it. And therefore "moved with fear, prepared an ark to the saving of his house," (Heb. 11:7). Nothing is more common with David than to put faith and fear together, "taste and see that the LORD is good: blessed is the man that trusteth in him. O fear the LORD, ye his saints: for there is no want to them that fear him," (Psa. 34:8, 9). The promises are made to fear. If therefore you fear God, you may on that ground believe that God will make his promises good to you. You shall find fear, joy, and faith linked together in in Psalm 64:9-10, "And all men shall fear...God...The righteous shall be glad in the LORD, and shall trust in him." Therefore,

the righteous fear God because they believe that God is just and powerful. And therefore many do not fear God, because they do not believe. Besides, he that steadfastly believes that God will save him, will not therefore presume, but fear to dishonor so gracious a God.

4. Fear and hope kiss each other also. "Every man that hath this hope purifieth himself," (1 John 3:3), that is, he fears to present his God with an unpurified heart. No man thinks that that man hopes to rise who does not fear to vex, cross, and abuse his prince. A loyal subject who fears to move his prince is the man of hopes. And therefore David chains fear and hope together. "The eye of the Lord is upon them that fear him, upon them that hope in his mercy," (Psa. 33:18). And again, "the Lord takes pleasure in those that fear him, in those that hope in his mercy," (Psa. 147:11).

If the soul triumphs then in the chariot of grace, where love, joy, and hope are three of the wheels, I do not know why the fear God may not be the fourth wheel. The soul standing on the four is like a four square stone, which way so ever you cast it, it falls right.

CHAPTER 6

How far the filial fear of God may stand with the fear of Man.

The filial fear of God may *stand*,

1. With the fear of reverence, due to men, as they are subordinate to God, as they are deputies of God on earth. God allows that the son should honor his father, and the servant his master; and on this very ground he challenges fear and honor to himself. He says, "if then I be a father, where is mine honour? and if I be a master, where is my fear?" (Mal. 1:6). This fear of man St. Paul imposes on us all, "Render...to all their dues...fear to whom fear, honour to whom honour," (Romans 13:7). His reason is in the foregoing verse, for they are God's ministers (Rom. 13:4). He cannot fear and reverence God who does not fear and reverence those that are God's substitutes. And therefore Solomon knew what he did when he put these two duties together, "My son, fear thou the Lord and the king," (Prov. 24:21). Fear the Lord first, and most; but yet fear the king too, who is God's vicegerent on earth. These two are not like the Ark of the Covenant and Dagon, they will both stand under the roof of one heart. Who feared God more than David, and yet who feared King Saul more than David? His heart smote him for cutting off but the skirt of King Saul's

garment (1 Sam. 24:4-5). Let the Pope, whose religion is rebellion and whose faith is faction, persuade his misled fools and his sworn slaves that, to fear God and to kill kings at his command are two virtues of one house (*cf.* the *Form of Prayer* on November 5th, page 58). They whose religion is from above, pure and peaceable, know that light and darkness, heaven and hell, God and the devil may as well have no fellowship together. The fear of God neither makes void, nor weakens this fear of observance towards man; but rather confirms and establishes it.

2. We may filially fear God, and yet fear man with a fear of caution. That is, we may fear the persecution and the society of evil men.

1. We may fear their persecutions, our Savior will justify us in it. He says, "Behold, I send you forth as sheep in the midst of wolves: be ye therefore wise as serpents...[and] beware of men: for they will deliver you up to the councils, and they will scourge you in their synagogues...But when they persecute you in this city, flee ye into another," (Matt. 10:16, 17, 23). Moses fled from Pharaoh, David from Saul, Elijah from Jezebel; no, our Savior himself from the Jews, when they would have cast him down a hill (Luke 4:29-30). When Athanasius was persecuted by the Arians, he made this motion to his friends, "Let us step aside for a time, until this

tempest be overpast: it will not be long before this little cloud vanishes." (*Secedamus ad tempus muleculaesl quecito evanescet.*) And when his persecutors upbraided him with his flight, he returned this answer to them, "If it be a shame for me to fly, it is a greater shame for you to persecute me." Thus we may fear persecution.

2. We may fear the society of bad men, both for the infection and the danger of it.

1. We have just cause to fear the contagion of ill company. Seneca says, "When I have been among men, I return from them more inhumane." Christ says, "Beware of false prophets, which come to you in sheep's clothing, but inwardly they are ravening wolves," (Matt. 7:15). Like our sneaking Mass priests that pretend a pity towards our souls, but their end is to make us sevenfold more the children of the devil. Gregory says that heretics act as seducers under the habits of counselors. And of such Saint Paul forewarns and gives us their character, "Traitors, heady, highminded...having a form of godliness, but denying the power thereof: from such turn away," (2 Tim. 3:4-5).

2. We have authority for fearing as the infection, so the danger of ill society by no less a voice from heaven, "Come out [from Babylon] my people, that ye be not partakers of her sins...[and] of her plagues," (Rev. 18:4). We read in

ecclesiastical history that St. John the Apostle being in a bath at Ephesus where in Cerinthus, a grand heretic, was bathing himself, he leaped out of the bath, as if he had spied a serpent, and with these words in his mouth, "I fear lest the ground should sink under me, whereon such a mortal enemy of the truth stands."

So then, the fear of God may stand with; no, what if I say it cannot stand without this kind of fear of men?

Besides, I must add, to prevent all mistake, that God's dearest saints and servants may be tempted, though not habitually, yet actually to fear man more than God.

The fear of man moved Abraham to deny his wife Sarah, so that she might have been exposed to Abimelech's lust (Gen. 20:2). The fear of King Saul moved Samuel to refuse to go at God's command to anoint David King (1 Sam. 16:1-2). David's fear of Achish moved him to the dishonor both of religion and manhood, to fain himself mad, to scrabble on the doors, and to let his spittle fall on his beard before King Achish (1 Sam. 21:12, 13). Jonah the Prophet's fear of the Ninevites moved him, when he was sent by God one way, to fly another way (Jon. 1:2, 3). The fear of man moved Peter to deny Christ his master with an oath, and a bitter execration (Matt. 26:69-72).

And yet when the Saints so fear *men*,

1. The Spirit of the fear of God has residence in them. Those that are in heaven are all spirit and no flesh. The wicked on earth are all flesh and no spirit. The saints on earth are partly flesh and partly spirit. New converts are more flesh, less spirit. Ancient standers in the school of Grace are more spirit, less flesh. In all the faithful there is a combat between the flesh and the spirit (Gal. 5:17). The flesh and the spirit are contrary to each other so that we cannot do the things that we would. The spirit is willing, but the flesh is weak. A Christian between these two is like a piece of iron between two loadstones: The one draws one way, and the other, the other way. Like a horse under an unskillful rider that spurs him in, sometimes the spirit has the better of the flesh; sometimes the flesh has the upper hand of the spirit. Sometimes the carnal fear of man prevails against the filial fear of God. When the saints are thus shaken and winnowed by the relics of sin in them, and by the temptation of Satan, they are not hereby proved to be chaff, though it appears that they are not without chaff.

2. As this fear of men in good men is not separated from the true fear of God, so neither from the true loved of God. When St. Peter denied Christ, he did not hate Christ, only he loved himself too much, Saint Bernard says. It is one thing for a man to fall through the fear of the world, but

another thing to fall through the love of the world. For he that loves the world, hates God, if we believe St. James (Jam. 4:4). But he that sometimes over-fears the world, may yet both dearly love, and sincerely fear God.

3. When he that fears God over-fears man, he does not do so with the uninterrupted swing of his affection; but he resists this carnal fear, and heartily desires that it were wholly expelled, and that the fear of God in him would be perfect, and unmixed. "Thy servants desire to fear thy name," says Nehemiah (Neh. 1:11). The fear of man in them is a tyrant that forces their subjection, not their King, to whom they freely yield their homage.

4. When the filial fearers of God fall by the fear of men, they fall not because of premeditation, but suddenly, being surprised by temptation unawares. The devil takes them at an unexpected advantage. The storm comes before they have leisure to snatch their cloak about them. As a valiant man may startle at the sudden discharge of a bullet from his gun behind his back; who otherwise having time to collect and summon his spirits, would not fear to stand at the mouth of a charged canon in good cause. Saint Peter was challenged by the damsel suddenly, before he could respite to reach his weapon of faith to draw it. Where, had he never so little time to have

recollected himself, his tongue would never have so grossly transgressed its bounds.

5. Though a child of God presently is scared by man, yet let him alone a while, and he will return to his true temper. He will recover his guard again, and his spiritual will shall conquer his carnal fear. As if you shake the compass, the needle may be turned from the north, but let the compass stand still a while and then the needle will point full toward the North Star. The most skillful pilot may, in a storm, be forced from his intended scope and port –who when the winds are silenced—will steer right course again. Put oil and water into a glass together, shake the glass and, though the water may get uppermost, let the glass stand a while, and the oil will, like a triumphant liquor, recover the superiority again. Though Saint Peter in the time of temptation denied his master, yet soon after when he came to himself, he wept bitterly for it. And after he confessed Christ stoutly before a council who before denied Him before a Damsel, he sealed his profession with his blood. Ecebolius, who in Julian's time, revolted from the truth for fear of man, did afterward cast himself down in the sight of all, cried in their hearing, "Kick me unsavory salt."[4] Archbishop Cranmer, who for fear had subscribed to many popish articles, afterwards suffered for

---

[4] *Calcate me salem insipidum.*

the truth, and he first thrust that hand into the flame wherewith he had subscribed. Thus, as it was said of Gad, "A troop shall overcome him, but he shall overcome at last," (Gen. 49:19). So fleshly fear may for a time overcome a fear of God, but he who filially fears God shall overcome at the last.

CHAPTER 7

Whether the fear of judgment is contrary to the filial

fear of God?

This doubt we resolve negatively:

For first, it is but natural to fear that that is contrary to nature. Though grace is above nature, yet it is not contrary to nature.

2. The best saints have stood in awe of God's judgments and their fear is recorded in holy Scripture to their praise. "My flesh trembleth for fear of thee; and I am afraid of thy judgments," David says (Psa. 119:120). The Prophet says, "When I heard, my belly trembled; my lips quivered...Rottenness entered into my bones," (Hab. 3:16).

3. There is much good included in the fear of God's *judgments*:

For first, it softens and melts the heart; the heart of the king of Judah was tender when he heard God's threatenings (2 Chro. 34:27).

2. This fear humbles the soul and lays a man low in his own eyes. "Put them in fear, O Lord: that the nations may know themselves to be but men," David says (Psa. 9:20). Through the fear of the majesty and the judgments of God,

"the lofty looks of man shall be humbled, and the haughtiness of men shall be bowed down," (Isa. 2:10-11).

3. This fear prevents the commission of many sins. Laban would have troubled Jacob, but he dared not (Gen. 31:29). Balaam would have cursed the people of God if he had dared to, but the Angel of the Lord met him with a drawn sword and intercepted his purpose (Num. 22:33-34). So the fear of judgment is a softener, a humbler, a preventer of sin. It softens the heart as fire dissolves the most solid, hardest metal. It humbles the heart as thunder lays prostrate to the tallest, stoutest cedars. It prevents much mischief, and so it is like a hedge of thorns in a man's way to keep him from breaking his bounds (Hos. 2:6).

Therefore this fear is not evil in itself, but good and necessary. For if rulers are to be feared because they are ministers to execute vengeance upon evil doers (Rom. 13:4), then God is much more to be feared for his vengeance, according to that of the Apostle, "serve God acceptably with reverence and godly fear: For our God is a consuming fire," (Heb. 12:28-29).

CHAPTER 8

The proper distinguishable symptoms of the fear of
God. And first of those absolute signs that discover the
essential ingredients that constitute the genuine fear of
God.

These signs are many. Give me leave to present the reader with the picture in great of him who fears God; and yet I shall be compelled, through the variety and fullness of this subject, to do as they that draw maps of the world, who set down a line for a river, and a spot for a whole country.

1. They that fear God have a high, reverent, awful, respective estimation both of God and of his ordinances.

"That thou mayest fear this glorious and fearful name, THE LORD THY GOD," says Moses (Deut. 28:58). That is for reverence toward the name of God.

"With fear you received Titus," (2 Cor. 7:15); that is, with respect and reverence, says Paul. There is reverence toward the ministers of God.

"And Jacob awaked out of his sleep (*in the place where God spake to him in a dream*) and he said, Surely the Lord is in this place; and I knew it not. And he was afraid, and said, How dreadful is this place! This is none other but the house of

God, and this is the gate of heaven," (Gen. 28:16-17). That is for reverence in the place, wherein God shall be pleased to manifest himself to us, and more specifically the Church, the congregation of the saints.

He that fears God will not be rash to utter anything before God, because he sees and acknowledges such a vast distance between God and him; God being in heaven, and he being on earth (Eccl. 5:2). As Solomon says in his book of retractions, he that fears God, fears before God (Eccl. 8:12, 13), that is, in the presence of God, which is most manifest, and constant in his holy temple. "The Lord is in his holy temple," David says (Psa. 11:4). Though his throne is in heaven, the temple is his house, his court, as David describes it (Psa. 84:1, 2, 4). This was David's fear, "I will come into thy house...and in thy fear will I worship toward thy holy temple," (Psa. 5:7). This was the fear of Levi, God says of him, "he...was afraid before my name," (Mal. 2:5). That is, he was reverent in my worship. And therefore these two are joined together in St. John, "Fear God, and give glory to him...and worship him," (Rev. 14:7). To glorify God in a reverent worshiping of him is to fear God. It is the song of the saints in heaven "who shall not fear thee, O Lord, and glorify thy name...for all nations shall come and worship before thee," (Rev. 15:4).

To sum it up, it amounts to this: he that fears God, reverences the name of God, honors the messengers of God, and behaves himself reverently in the place of God's worship. In the parts of God's worship, in prayer, in preaching, in hearing, in administering and participating in the holy sacrament. On the other side, he that can blasphemously toss and tear the awful name of God by hellish swearing, and devilish cursing; he that can take the sacred name of God into his mouth when there is little or no thought of it in his heart (Isa. 29:13); he that disesteems, undervalues, despises, scorns, and mocks the messengers of God; he that puts no difference between God's house and his own, between the sacramental bread and wine consecrated to configure such mysteries from that of common bread and wine (1 Cor. 11:22); he that can willingly sleep or otherwise without regard, drowsily demeans himself in the service of his God (1 Cor. 11:29); he has no fear of God before his eyes.

2. He that fears God will thirst to be fully acquainted with the whole will of God, so that through ignorance or mistake, he may neither neglect what God commands, nor do what he forbids, nor do amiss, nor overdo anything. This is called proving or searching what is the good and acceptable will of God, what he accepts, what he dislikes (Rom. 12:2). It was King David's prayers, "Teach me thy way, O Lord...unite

my heart to fear thy name," (Psa. 86:11). He manifests his desire to fear God by desiring that God would teach him his way. This he requests more than once in one Psalm, "Teach me thy statutes," (Psa. 119:12, 26, 33). As that son that fears his father will punctually inquire into his father's disposition as to what he likes, or what displeases him. But he takes no care to build himself in the knowledge of the will of God, but contents himself with ignorance; no, it may be, winks against the light, the beams of which would otherwise dart into and irradiate upon his soul, on purpose that he might sin more freely, without check of conscience, which being enlightened, would do its office in accusing. That man does not fear God. Of this stamp were those of which Job speaks of who said to God, "we desire not the knowledge of thy ways," (Job 21:14) and that "say to the seers, See not, and to the prophets, Prophesy not unto us right things, speak unto us smooth things," (Isa. 30:10). As if they should say, "Do you expect us to thank you for preaching freely and frequently? We wish you would preach less and gives us better content." David says, "There is no fear of God before [*the wicked man's*] eyes," (Psa. 36:1). How does that appear? By this he flatters himself (Psa. 36:2), he desires to be flattered. He would willingly know the plain truth. He loves to drink in troubled waters, that he might not see his own deformity, nor understand his duty.

3. He that fears God has a soft, melting, yielding, pliable heart to all good impressions. Job says, "I am afraid of [God], for [he] maketh my heart soft," (Job 23:14, 15). But he that has a brow of brass (Isa. 48:4), a whore's forehead (Jer. 3:3), an iron sinew, an unbreakable heart, a perverse thwart, cross will, that neither has, nor promises, neither mercies nor judgments, can dissolve, or mollify. That man owns not the fear of God. Therefore, it is that fear of God and hardness of heart are opposed to one another by Solomon, "Happy is the man that feareth always, but he that hardeneth his heart shall fall into mischief," (Pro. 28:14). Our hearts are "hardened...from thy fear," says the Prophet (Isa. 63:17).

4. He that fears God will tremble at God's threatenings in his word. This is poverty and contriteness of spirit to tremble at God's word as it is in Isaiah. 66:2. Habakkuk says, "When I heard, my belly trembled; my lips quivered...rottenness entered into my bones," (Hab. 3:16). When Micah prophesied of the destruction of Jerusalem, King Hezekiah feared the Lord, and besought him to avert the evil (Jer. 26:18, 19). When Baruch read the book of God's threatenings in the ears of the princes, the text says they were "afraid both one and other," (Jer. 36:15, 16).

But he that hearing the words of this book of God, blesses himself in his heart (Deut. 29:19), and promises himself peace and safety (1 Thess. 5:3), and puts from him the evil day (Amos 6:3). He that thinks pulpit threats to be bogeymen and scarecrows to frighten children with, and is no more moved with them than the seat he sits on, that man has no fear of God before his eyes.

5. He that truly fears God is in love with the fear of God, he rejoices in it, he cherishes it, he wishes the increase of it. The saints "desire to fear thy name," says Nehemiah (Neh. 1:11). "Thy servant is devoted to thy fear," says the sweet singer of Israel (Psa. 119:38). But he that resolves to lead a merry life, to take nothing to heart, to sing care away, and to stop the mouth of conscience when it chides, he does not know experimentally what the fear of God means.

6. He that fears God, when he conceives he has provoked God to anger, never ceases praying, entreating the prayers of others, interposing the merits of Christ between every word of his prayer, his heart is never at rest, until his peace is made with God, until he finds God reconciled to him. Thus David lively expressed his fear of God saying, "According unto the multitude of thy tender mercies blot out my transgressions, wash me thoroughly from mine iniquity, and cleanse me from my sin...cast me not away from thy

presence...make me to hear joy and gladness; that the bones which thou hast broken may rejoice...restore unto me the joy of thy salvation," (Psa. 51:1, 2, 8, 11-12) and, "How long...wilt thou hide thyself forever? shall thy wrath burn like fire?...Lord, where are thy former lovingkindnesses?" (Psa. 89:46, 49).

But he that, because sentence against sin is not speedily executed, sets his heart to do evil (Eccl. 8:11-12), and thinks that God has forgotten, and so runs on the score, and never thinks of agreeing with his maker, and making up the breach, he is a stranger to the fear of God.

7. He that fears God doth at all times, and in all places, set himself as in the presence of God. As David set God always before his eyes (Psa. 16:8). "Thou knowest...my thoughts afar off...there is not a word in my tongue, but, lo, O Lord, thou knowest it altogether...whither shall I flee from thy presence?" (Psa. 139:2, 4, 7-9). Fear quickens the memory: nothing more dwells in our thoughts than that person or thing that we most love or fear. He that fears God always "sees him who is invisible," (Heb. 11:27).[5] He conceives that God is always present, as if he saw his very essence. He says, especially in solemn conventions and actions as Cornelius did, "Now are we all here present before God," (Acts 10:33). But he in whose

---

[5] Heb. 11:27, ἀόρατον ὡς ὁρῶν. *Sec semper deum presentem intelligit, ac so insua assentta, viderat.* Bernard, form. Bon. Vit. Acts 10:33, Psal 10:4.

thoughts God is not resident (Psa. 10:4), he is as far from the fear of God as the thought of God.

8. He that fears God has a quick eye to discern when God is displeased, and he is grieved at the heart when God's honor is impeached either by himself, or others. He grieves for his own sins, and "Ephraim bemoaning himself thus...After that I was instructed, I smote upon my thigh. I was ashamed, yea, even confounded," (Jer. 31:18, 19). And as David cried out in the bitterness of his heart, "Against thee, thee only, have I sinned," (Psa. 51:4). He had sinned against Uriah, against Bathsheba, against Israel, but he is most sensible of his offending of God.

Again, he that fears God grieves when others are injurious to God's glory. "Rivers of water run down mine eyes, because they keep not thy law," (Psa. 119:136). "Horror hath taken hold upon me because of the wicked that forsake thy law," (Psa. 119:53). He that fears God will tremble to hear another lie, and swear, and curse, and provoke God. But he that is neither moved with his own, nor with other men's sins, but makes the one his pride, and the other his mirth, how can the fear of God dwell in that man?

9. He that fears God will be careful for the future to avoid whatsoever may prove offensive to God. And therefore David puts these together, "Stand in awe, and sin not," (Psa.

4:4). And therefore he says, "The fear of the Lord is clean" (Psa. 19:9), because it keeps men's hearts and hands clean. "The fear of the Lord is to hate evil" (Prov. 8:13), and "by the fear of the Lord men depart from evil," says Solomon (Prov. 6:16). He that fears God, fears sin. It is part of the description of a good man in Ecclesiastes that he "feareth an oath," (Eccl. 9:2). And so I say of other sins. No, he fears sin when time, place, and opportunity do woo him to it. As Joseph would not yield to his mistress's lust, though there was no fear of discovery, all his argument was, "How then can I do this great wickedness, and sin against God?" (Gen. 39:9). But he that passes not how much God is displeased, so he may please, humor, and satisfy his own lust, his heart is not possessed with the fear of God.

10. He that fears God will study in all things to please God. He will obey God conscionably and constantly. And therefore to fear God, and to keep his commandments, are put together by the wise man (Eccl. 12:13). It is said of the centurion that he "feared God" and was "a devout man...gave much alms...and prayed," (Acts 10:2). "Serve the Lord with fear," David says (Psa. 2:11). He that serves God, fears him, and he that fears him, will serve him. They cannot be disjoined.

If you make no conscience of diligent service to God, both in your general and particular calling, and of serving him in that manner that he desires to be served in, never say that you fear God.

Lastly, he that fears God will not willingly wrong his neighbor, neither in word or deed. Joseph said to his brothers, "This do, and live; for I fear God," (Gen. 42:18). That is, I will keep my promise with you, if you perform the condition, for I fear God, and therefore I dare not be a promise-breaker. The Hebrew midwives would not kill the male children at the King's command because, "they feared God," (Exod. 1:17). And the Law of God runs this way, "Thou shalt not curse the deaf, nor put a stumbling-block before the blind, but shalt fear thy God," (Lev. 19:14). As if God should say, "If you fear me, you will not offer injury to your neighbor. No, not though you could escape the unknown. You will not curse him that cannot hear you, nor offend him that cannot see you to call you to account for it. "But the former governors that had been before me" oppressed the people, but "not I, because of the fear of God," (Neh. 5:15).

But he that makes no scruple of prejudicing and injuring superior, equal, inferior, any that may fall within his reach, he may call himself a servant of God, and a Christian, but as yet the fear of God has no place in his heart.

These are more simple and absolute signs of the fear of God considerable in itself.

CHAPTER 9

Of those signs that put a difference between the slavish,

and the filial fear of God.

The slavish and the son-like kindly fear of God *differ*:

1. In their several grounds and principles,

1. The slavish fear is awakened only by threatenings denounced by God against disobedience. This moved King Abimelech to restore Sara to Abraham; God in a dream signified to him that if he did not restore her, he and all his should die for it (Gen. 20:6-7). When Jonah had cried, "Forty days, and Nineveh shall be overthrown," (Jonah 3:4), then they were amazed, and fasted and prayed. On the other side, the filial fear of God will be awaked by the mere commandment of God, though there is no threatening associated with it. This Solomon calls, "fearing the commandment," (Prov. 13:13); that is, fearing not to do what is commanded merely because it is commanded, and fearing to do what is forbidden, because it is forbidden, though the commandment is not supported by way of sanction of promise or threatening.

2. The slavish fear is stirred up only by judgments inflicted on men's selves or on others. Asaph says, "Thou didst cause judgment to be heard from heaven; the earth feared."

Whereas filial fear is excited by the mercy and loving-kindness of God. "There is mercy with thee, that thou mayest be feared," (Psa. 130:4). The prophet says they "shall fear the Lord and his goodness," (Hos. 3:5). "God will not afflict," says Job, "Men do therefore fear him," (Job. 37:23, 24). What men? Certainly not slaves, but loving and loyal sons.

2. Slavish and filial fear differ in their objects. *For,*

1. The object of slavish fear is not sin, but punishment. As children fear a coal only when it burns, but otherwise whatever is never so black, they will delight to handle it. So Balaam did not fear to curse God's people, but he feared the Angel that met him in the way with a drawn sword (Num. 22:31-32).

But the object of filial fear is sin, though there is no plagues in store here, nor no hell hereafter for the offender. Solomon says, "The righteous...feareth an oath," (Eccl. 9:2). That is, he so much fears the curse of the flying book that shall enter into the house of the swearer, as he fears the oath itself. He fears more to swear, than that God should swear in his wrath against him (Psa. 95:11). He fears more to curse then to be cursed, to hate than to be hated, to injure than to be injured. He fears more active, than passive evil. Like that woman in the hieroglyphic, that having a firebrand in one hand and a pot of water in the other, is presented, wishing that with that firebrand she could dry up the waters of Paradise; and with that water quench the flames of hell, that she might serve God, neither for hopes of heaven, nor for fear of hell.

2. If the object of slavish fear is sin, yet it is only sin of the grosser size, of a scarlet dye. As the Pharisees feared to swallow camels, but gnats would go down well enough (Matt. 23:24). And among Christians, many fear the more horrid oaths, but the lesser does not bother them. Many fear to kill a man who do not fear to hate, backbite, or curse him, which is murder in a degree, as our Savior reckons it in his Sermon on the Mount (Matt. 5:21, 22).

But on the other side, they that filially fear God, fear those sins that seem least, as idle words and vain thoughts. David feared the cutting of the lap of Saul's garment (1 Sam. 24:4, 5). Job feared to look upon a maid lustfully (Job 31:1). Saint Austin feared the stealing of a few apples (see his *Confession*). John Hus feared lest he should spend too much time at playing chess. The truly fearful are jealous over themselves in the use of indifferences, lest in tasting of the honey of them, they should, like a fly, stick in the slime.

Let every man apply this trial to himself.

3. Slavish and filial fear differ in their consequences and effects. *For,*

1. Slavish fear dulls and deadens a man's heart, so that he is fit for no good thing. It made Nabal's heart die within him, so that he became as a stone (1 Sam. 25:37). When God rebuked and spoiled the wicked, they fell into a fear, so that none of them found their hands, but they were cast into a dead sleep, David says (Psa. 76:5-6, 8). As when there was an earthquake at Christ's rising, and the angel's countenance was as lightning, the keepers for fear shook, and became as dead men (Matt. 28:4).

But filial fear makes such as are endued with it lively and active in their duty. Thus Noah being "moved with fear," did not sit sill, but "prepared an ark," (Heb. 11:7). And indeed this is God's command. Moses says, "What doth the Lord thy God require of thee, but to fear the Lord thy God, to walk in all his ways?" (Deut. 10:12). Filial fear does not make a man lame in his duty, but sets him upon his legs.

2. If slavish fear moves a man to do any good, it will be only so much as the fearer thinks will serve him, and no more. He will give God but gold weight; very hard measure. But filial fear will make a man to strive after perfection, to press hard forward to the mark of the high calling. And therefore Saint Paul's exhortations runs, "Perfect holiness in the fear of God," (2 Cor. 7:1) and "Work out your salvation with fear and trembling," (Phil. 2:12). If you fear God, you will not work by

halves, but work out your salvation. Not that merit of justification by works is admitted by us. The phrase "fear and trembling" excludes that. To fear and to be self-confident are antithetical, they cannot stand together.

3. Slavish fear curbs sin, it may make a dam against it, it may prune or lop it, but it does not mortify sin in the power and love of it. This fear is like the quaking of a rotten quagmire. The wolf may fear to come to the flock, yet he loves the blood of sheep no less. But he that filially fears God, not only avoids it, but also hates sin. Solomon says, "The fear of the Lord is to hate evil," (Pro. 8:13). In the worst of men through the fear of punishment, the faculties indeed may be bridled; but in those that filially fear God, the will is healed.

4. Slavish fear fills the heart with distraction and distrust. It made Lot fearful that he should be consumed between Sodom and the mountain, though God had promised him his life if he hastened (Gen. 19:19). It made the people deny to go up to Canaan because of the multitude and strength of the inhabitants, though God had promised them conquest over the Canaanites and the possession of the land (Num. 13:2-31). It spurred Cain and Judas to despair. It did not lead Judas to the Lord, but it drew him to the halter. But the filial fear of God is never without faith in God, as has been proven. "Though I walk through the valley of the shadow of

death, I will fear no evil, for thou art with me," (Psa. 23:4). And again, they that "fear God will trust in him," (Psa. 64:9-10). The kindly fear of God does not disjoint, but consolidates, settles, and balances the heart amidst all inward and outward storms and tempests.

5. The slavish fear of God is usually joined with hatred of God in some degree. It was the speech of a tyrant: "Let the people hate me, so they fear me." This fear wishes there were no God, or that he could not see, or not be able to punish sin. But the filial fear of God is never disjoined from the fervent unfeigned love of God. They that fear God, and they that love God, are put in the same description by the Psalmist, and they are interested in the same promises, that their prayers shall be heard, desires fulfilled, they shall be preserved and saved (Psa. 145:19, 20). And God in the Law requires fear and love united together (Deut. 10:12). They that fear God, love God, because they are beloved of God. For David calls the fearers of God, God's beloved (Psa. 60:4, 5). And we love God "because he first loved us," John says (1 John 4:19).

6. Slavish fear drives men from God. We see it in our grandfather Adam. He confesses that being afraid, he hid himself among the trees of the garden (Gen. 3:8-10). The Prophet says, "And they shall go into the holes of the rocks, and into the caves of the earth, for fear of the Lord, and for the

glory of his majesty, when he ariseth to shake terribly the earth," (Isa. 2:19). Saint John says that men will say "to the mountains and rocks, Fall on us, and hide us from the face of him that sitteth on the throne," (Rev. 6:16). This fear does not care how far God and it are apart. Like that fear of the Egyptians, Egypt was glad of the Israelites' departure for they were afraid of them (Psa. 105:38). But the filial fear of God unites the heart to God. It drives him who is possessed of it unto God. When David was in a difficult spot he cries, "Let us fall into the hand of the Lord," (2 Sam. 24:14). And it is God's promise, "I will put my fear in their hearts, that they shall not depart from me," (Jer. 32:40). The fear of a slave provokes him to run from his master; the fear of a loving child prompts him to apply himself all the closer to his father. In these six effects, these two fears are differed.

4. And lastly, they differ in regard of time and duration. To wind them up together, slavish fear does not dread God in prosperity, when all things smile, and succeed according to our expectation and wish. "Because the wicked have no changes," says the Psalmist, "therefore they fear not God," (Psa. 55:19).

He that filially fears God, fears him at all times. You may imagine it to be a misery, a bondage, to be always in fear, but the contrary is true of this fear. "Happy is the man that feareth always," says Solomon (Pro. 28:14). The righteous man does not fear God by fits and starts. He fears most when he is most prosperous. He thinks that the greatest calms are but fatal and immediate forerunners of the worst tempests. When the churches had rest and comfort in the Holy Spirit, even then they walked in the fear of the Lord (Acts 9:31). They think with St. Bernard, when they are spared too long, that then God is most angry when he seems least angry. When they sin unpunished they cry with St. Austin, "Lord let me have none of this mercy, lest it prove but a reservation of me to great misery."

In a word, he that fears God slavishly fears little longer than the rod is on his back. It was the guise of kings Pharaoh and Ahab, when the pang was off, they still hardened their hearts and ran their old bias (1 Kings 21:27-29). We find Ahab fasting and humbling himself in one chapter, and the next news we hear of him, he is quarreling with the Prophet for telling the truth (1 Kings 22:18, 19). No, this fear turns into a greater security, as the anvil is harder for beating, as hot water cooling, grows colder than it ever was before.

But the filial fear of God is a lasting fear; it "endures forever," David says (Psa. 19:9). The spirit of the fear of the Lord is not fleeting, it rests on him, on whom it pitches (Isa. 11:2). Let us all look at our reflection in this mirror, it is no flattering one, it will tell you truly whether your fear is of the right stamp, whether it will stand with you, instead, or not.

CHAPTER 10

Of those signs that discover whether we fear God more

than man, or man more than God.

There are signs of a third rank that will make a full discovery to us, whether we fear man more than God, or God more than man.

1. They that study more to please man than to please God, they that do not pass to displease God so that they humor men, they fear man more than God. "If I yet pleased men, I should not be the servant of Christ," (Gal. 2:10). As if he should say, I cannot fear Christ as a servant should fear his master, if I seek to please men. Would any of you judge that a servant fears his master more than other men, if his daily care were to please other men rather than his master? It is not for nothing that Saint Paul opposes man-pleasing to fearing of God, implying that light and darkness can as well consist together as sycophantic, slavish pleasing of man can stand with the fear of God. Who doubts but that, at that time, Aaron feared man more than God when, to condescend to the people, he made them gods for them to worship in Moses' absence (Exod. 32:22-24)? Whether Pilate feared God or man most when, to content the people, he released Barabbas and delivered Jesus to be crucified (Mark 15:15)? When Herod the

King vexed the church of God and killed James with the sword, and because he saw it pleased the Jews, he proceeded further to take Peter also, as is written of him (Acts 12:1-3); will any man say that Herod feared God more than man? On the contrary part, they that fear God more than man, though in all indifferent things he will please men, as St. Paul testifies of himself, "Even as I please all men in all things," (that is, in all lawful things, for "the profit of many, that they may be saved," (1 Cor. 10:33). "I became as a Jew, that I might gain the Jews; to them that are under the law, as under the law, that I might gain them that are under the law; To them that are without law, as without law...that I might gain them...to the weak became I as weak...I am made all things to all men, that I might by all means save some," (1 Cor. 9:20-22). Yet in those things that are neither harmful or beneficial, indifferent, but either necessary, or unlawful, they will not yield a hair's breadth, though to please the greatest, and their best benefactors. And therefore the question of those that fear God is not what man, but what God will be pleased with, as it was their question (though with other intention) in the Prophet, "Will the Lord be pleased with thousands of rams, or with ten thousands of rivers of oil?" (Micah 6:7). Paul says we speak "not as pleasing men, but God, which trieth our hearts," (1 Thess. 2:4). That preacher who fears God more than man, will in the pulpit speak his conscience, with modesty and good discretion, even to the faces of the highest *grandees* and *magnificoes* of the world, though he knows it will prove harsh, unpleasant, and unwelcome to their ears. When King Ahab sent for Micaiah to prophesy to him, he was desired to speak as the prophets before him spoke, that which was good, and might please the King. His answer was, "As the Lord liveth, what the Lord saith unto me, that will I speak," (1 Kings 22:13, 14). As if he should say, "Do not tell me what other prophets have said. What God puts into my mouth, I will speak, is it good for the king or not, whether it please him or displease him. This was a fearer of God indeed.

1. They fear man more than God who will rather obey the commandment of man than of God. St. Paul says, "To whom ye yield yourselves servants to obey, his servants ye are to whom ye obey," (Rom. 6:16). That subject who will disobey God to obey a magistrate, that child who will disobey his Father in heaven to obey his earthly father, that servant who will disobey his heavenly master to obey his master according to the flesh (Eph. 6:5), that subject, that son, that servant fears man more than God. David says, "The transgression of the wicked saith within their heart, that there is no fear of God before his eyes," (Psa. 36:1). Where they that fear God more than man will infinitely prefer obedience to God before

subservience to man. None are more obedient to man than those that fear God, in what is agreeable with or not contrary to the will of God. But if God commands one thing, and man another, they desire to be pardoned if they take leave to obey the more supreme. And therefore when the council asked St. Peter and the other Apostles why they preached in the name of Jesus, when they had strict commands to the contrary, their answer was, "We ought to obey God rather than men," (Acts 5:28, 29). And when the council called them and commanded them not to preach in Christ's name, they returned with this answer, "Whether it be right in the sight of God to hearken unto you more than unto God, judge ye," (Acts 4:18-19).

3. They fear man more than God that would not abstain from sin, but only for the fear of man. Herod would have put John the Baptist to death, but he feared the multitude (Matt. 14:5). And the chief priests and Pharisees would have laid hands on Christ, but that they feared the people, who took Christ for a Prophet (Matt. 21:46). The captain and the officers brought the Apostles gently, and without violence, "for they feared the people, lest they should have been stoned," (Acts 5:26). Among us many fear stealing and murdering because they fear hanging. Many fear neglect of coming to church, and to communion, because they fear presenting themselves. Many fear adultery and fornication

because they fear discovery, the loss of their good name, and temporal fines. And what is all this but to fear man more than God? (*Oderunt peccare mali formiding paenae.*) On the other part, they that fear God more than man will fear to commit those sins on which the law of man takes no hold. For example, Job made a conscience decision of looking upon a maid to lust after (Job 31:1), a fault not liable to human censure.

4. They fear man more than God that will omit their duty, or commit any sin for the threats of men. "Of whom hast thou been afraid or feared, that thou has lied?" asks the Lord in Isaiah 57:11. Not of God, but of man. King Saul by his own confession, transgressed the commandment of the Lord because he feared the people (1 Sam. 15:24). Pope Marcelline, in the time of heathenish persecution, for fear of death, offered incense to devils, as he after confessed with grief, as many papists in their writings make mention.

On the contrary part, they that fear God more than man will not betray a tittle of truth to save their lives. They will die before they will yield so much as a knee in an idolatrous way, or without any part of God's worship from him, or in any kind make shipwreck of a good conscience. You find two famous examples here in the prophecy of Daniel. The one was this: Nebuchadnezzar threatened the three children, Shadrach, Meshach, and Abednego, that if at the sounding of the music they did not fall down and worship the golden image that he had set up, they should be cast in the hour of their refusal into the midst of a fiery furnace. But what answer did they return? This, "O Nebuchadnezzar, we are not careful to answer thee in this matter. If it be so, our God whom we serve is able to deliver us from the burning fiery furnace, and he will deliver us out of thine hand, O king. But if not, be it known unto thee, O king, that we will not serve thy gods, nor worship the golden image which thou has set up," (Dan. 3:15-18). A heroic resolution. The other example is this: King Darius sealed a decree that whosoever should ask a petition of any God or man for thirty days, he should be cast into the den of lions. Yet, for all this, Daniel knowing of the signing of this decree went into his house, opened his window toward Jerusalem, and kneeled upon his knees three times a day, and prayed to God (Dan. 6:7-10). He would not only not omit to pray, but he would not forbear the usual ceremonies in praying, of bowing the knee, and opening his window toward Jerusalem. So little the fear of man swayed him. Theoderet and Nazianzen relate of St. Basil, that he would say that "Those that feed upon God's word, will not suffer the least syllable of it to come into hazard. And again he would say, "We are in all other things modest and yielding, but when matters of faith and religion are in controversy, we are not timorous then, but as bold as lions. And again he would say to Modestus, a potent man, "Use all your power against me, you shall never persuade me to subscribe to your Arian heresy. These men feared God more than man. And we will not wonder that grace infuses such a courage into the fearers of God, when we shall hear the answers of Elvidius, Prsiscus, a heathen, to Vespasian the Emperor. The Emperor commanded him not to come on such a day to the Senate, or if he came to speak as he would have him. He answered that he was a Senator, and therefore it was fit that he should be at the Senate. And if being there, he were required by the rest to render his opinion, he must speak freely, and according to his conscience. The Emperor threatened him that he should die then. He replied that he knew he was not immoral, and he added, "Do what you will, I will do what I ought. It is in your power to kill me, but it is in my power to die constantly." Think but on this heathen, and then you will believe that grace can make the faithful much more spirited; they building upon better grounds than any heathen could. David says, "Princes did sit and speak against me: but thy servant did meditate in thy statutes," (Psa. 119:23). And again, "My soul is continually in thy hand: yet do I not forget thy law. The wicked have laid a snare for me: yet I erred not from thy precepts...Princes have persecuted me without a cause: but my heart standeth in awe of thy word," (Psa. 119:109, 110, 161). As if he should say, "I fear you more than any persecution."

5. They fear man more than God that in trouble fear man, and distrust God, and on the surprise of any evil, do not think on God, but of fortifying themselves by leagues with men. Such were they in the prophecy that looked after armor and walls, barriers and fortifications, but they had no respect to God (Isa. 22:8-11). They feared the enemy, but they did not dream of him whom they had provoked by their sins. But they that fear God more than man will be sure to make God sure, and for the rest they are fearless. David says, "What time I am afraid, I will trust in thee...I will not fear what flesh can do unto me," (Psa. 56:3, 4). And again, "Though an host should encamp against me, my heart shall not fear: though war should rise against me, in this will I be confident," (Psa. 27:3).

6. And lastly, they fear man more than God that forbear open sins that are obvious to human eyes, but make no conscience of secret sins, sins of the heart, of sins in darkness, or in retired places. Such, whose maxim is, "If not chastely, yet cautiously: No matter for keeping sin uncommitted, so you keep it unknown." This was the infirmity of Jacob. "My father peradventure will feel me, and I shall seem to him as a deceiver," (Gen. 27:12). His fear was not so much to be, as to seem a deceiver. But it is ordinary with wicked men. The

murdered kills while men are in bed. The adulterer waits for the twilight, and disguises his face. The thief digs through houses in the dark (Job 24:14-16). Paul says, "They that be drunken are drunken in the night," (1 Thess. 5:7). Though now these monsters confront the sun, God says, "Hast thou seen what the ancients of the house of Israel do in the dark, every man in the chambers of his imagery?" (Ezek. 8:12). And if every man had a window in his breast, or his thoughts were written in his forehead (as Cicero wished of every Roman), what monstrous counsels shall we be spectators of. On the contrary, they that fear God more than man will, with Joseph, refuse uncleanness, though they have opportunity and secrecy. They will not curse a deaf man that cannot hear them, nor cast a block before a blind man that cannot discover them. They will not curse their rulers, not in their bedchamber, not in their thoughts (Eccl. 10:20). This was Job's temper when he said he had not covered his transgressions, "Did I fear a great multitude, or did the contempt of families terrify me?" (Job 31:33, 34). No, he feared God more than man. Let us all try ourselves by this unerring rule.

CHAPTER 11

A dissuasion from those sins that are contrary to the

fear of God. And first of carnal security, with the

remedy of it.

That part of this treatise that is past is more doctrinal, what follows shall be more applicatory, either by way of dissuasion or exhortation.

The dissuasion part forbids all those sins that are contrary to the fear of God, and they are diverse; some of which are contrary to it excessively, and some in deficiency. I shall handle them in *order*:

1. One vice contrary to the fear of God is carnal security, a reckless carelessness: When men are moved neither with the threatenings of God in his Word, nor with the execution of God's judgments in the world, nor with the beginnings of God's wrath upon themselves. These are three heads of this *hydra*:

1. When men are not touched with the denouncing of the threatenings of God in his Word: Such are they that when they hear the words of God's curse, bless themselves in their hearts and say they shall have peace, although they walk according to the stubbornness of their own hearts, adding drunkenness to thirst, sin to sin, running around in the devil's

circle (Deut. 29:19, 20). Such as make a covenant with death, and agreement with hell, as if they should not faze them (Isa. 28:18).

Such as cry the vision is for many days to come, and the prophecy of the times that are afar off, the evil shall not fall in their days (Ezek. 12:27). Those that put away far from them the evil day as in Amos 6:3. Those that say in their hearts, the Lord will do neither good nor evil, as in Zephaniah 1:12. And are not most of our age this guise? Do we not say in our hearts, "Come, God will be better than his word. He that had made all will save all. Give the preachers leave to thunder, and lighten, we hope the best still, no man shall put us out of heart." If we were not lulled asleep in the cradle of security, how dare we touch that forbidden fruit that is guarded with angels (preachers I mean, for angel signifies a messenger) when they have a flaming sword in their mouths, threatening ruin to us? How dare we tear the sacred name of God when he has threatened that he will not hold him guiltless that takes his name in vain? How dare we distrust God's word, fear to defend a good cause, commit adultery, or lie, when God has menaced that all fearful, unbelieving, abominable, murderers, adulterers, and all liars shall have their part in the lake that burns with fire and brimstone (Rev. 21:8)? No, no, our transgression says to the entire world that there is no fear of God before our eyes, as David argues in Psalm 36:1.

2. It is carnal security not to be afraid when God has punished others for the same sins where we are deeply guilty; when our neighbor's house is on fire, not to fear our own. Such were the men of Laish, they dwelt carelessly and securely, as is recorded of them (Judges 18:7). And this is our crime. God's heavy rod has ridden circuit about other nations and our halcyon days of peace make us secure and careless. When a heathen can tell us, "When you are highest in stature, fear most." Evil is not confined to one people, it may go forth from nation to nation, as God says. The prophecies are filled with these expressions (Jer. 25:32). It is said in Ezekiel 32:10, "I will make many people amazed at thee, and their kings shall be horribly afraid for thee, when I shall brandish my sword before them; and they shall tremble at every moment, every man for his own life, in the day of thy fall." And yet we do not tremble, though God has long brandished his sword before our eyes in neighboring kingdoms. God may complain of us as he did of them in Zephaniah 3:6, 9, "I have cut off the nations...their cities are destroyed...I said, Surely thou wilt fear me, thou wilt receive instruction; so their dwelling should not be cut off...but they rose early, and corrupted all their doings." This is our case: the Lord help us, awaken us. As if we were

better than our neighbors, or more able to oppose our enemies, if God should let them in. I may take up that question to England, that God asked Nineveh, "Art thou better than populous? No, that was situated among the rivers...whose rampart was the sea? Ethiopia and Egypt were her strength...Yet was she carried away, she went into captivity," (Nahum 3:8-10). So may I say, O England, are you better than Germany, which now lies bleeding under desolation? If you are not better, why are you secure when she is ruined?

3. It is carnal security not to be terrified with the beginnings of God's wrath. And it may be said of us, as Salvian speaks of his times, "We have not only seen our neighbors burning, but we ourselves also have been scorched more than once, more than one way, and yet we fear not the flame." God has begun with us by sending the moth spoken of in Hosea 5:12, which moth insensibly eats out the heart of trading in England so that it was never at so dead. The time was (as it is in the Prophet) "when Ephraim spake trembling," (Hos. 13:1); so when England spoke, there was trembling, but now other nations slight us. We may say with David, God does "not go out with our armies," (Psa. 60:10). All this, wise men see and know and we are daily reminded of it, together with plagues, fevers, famines, droughts, and unseasonable seasons that we

have felt. And yet what man among us abates one drunken cup for all this? We are as jolly, as thoughtless, as secure, as if we were in the third heaven. We verify that that Antonius Pius spoke of the Christians that when earthquakes came, they were securest. This lethargy is too sure of our disease. I can run no better course to rouse us out of this leaden slumber, this sleep, than to prove that we are not the more, but the less safe for our security. And when our mischief arrives, it will be the more insufferable, the more unexpected it is. Will we believe God affirming it? He that "when he heareth the words of this curse, bless himself and promise to himself...peace...the Lord will not spare him, but then the anger of the Lord...shall smoke against the man, and all the curses that are written in this book shall lie upon him, and the Lord shall blot out his name from under heaven," (Deut. 29:19, 20). They "that put far away the evil day...shall they go captive with the first that go captive," (Amos 6:3, 7). The rich man in the gospel said to his soul, "Soul, thou hast much goods laid up for many years, take thine ease, eat, drink, and be merry." But there came a fearful message from heaven to him, "Thou fool, this night thy soul shall be required of thee: then whose shall those things be, which thou hast provided?" (Luke 12:19-20). It was the old world's case in the days of Noah (Matt. 24:38-39), they were eating and drinking, marrying and giving in marriage, until the day that Noah entered into the Ark, and they did not know, until the flood came, and took them all away. And such shall Christ's second coming be, like a snare it shall fall upon the world when they least think of it, when they are drowned in security. "When they shall say, Peace and safety; then sudden destruction cometh upon them, as travail upon a woman with child," says the Apostle (1 Thess. 5:3). And it is a prophecy of these latter days, we may sleep and snort in our sins, but our "damnation slumbereth not," says Peter (2 Peter 2:3). This is the voice of the Scripture. And the Father speaks the same language. They were as cocks to awake these drowsy times. St. Augustine says, "Security is the forerunner of certain ruin. He that promises himself peace in an unlawful course of life, shall be invaded when he least suspects it.[6] "Fear is taken from the wicked that they might not be aware when judgment seizeth them," says Salvian, *Ablatus peccatoribus tenor ne posset esse cautcla.* No, the glimmering light of the heathen, discovered this truth to them. "Men used to be most secure when the greatest evils hang over their heads," Seneca the Tragedian says.[7] "When all things seem quiet, that which is noxious is not absent, though it be silent," says Seneca the Philosopher.

---

[6] *Certe ruinae pravia est incuria Qui siht pacem promnitut, secures modunar,* Aug. in Psa. 130. *Ablatus di peccatoribus tumor, ne pesset esse cautela* Salv.

[7] *Solent suprema faceresecuros mala.* Oedip. 2.2.

Nature will teach us that the air is always calm before an earthquake, and there is usually lightning before death.

Little thought Corah, Dathan, and Abiram when they rebelled against Moses, that the earth would swallow them quick; they were gazing at the doors of their tents (Num. 16:31, 32).

Little thought Zimri and Cosbi to be both thrust through the belly in the act of adultery (Num. 25:8). Little thought Agag the King of the Amalekites to be hewn in pieces by Samuel's sword when he came in delicately and said, "Surely the bitterness of death is past," (1 Sam. 15:32-33).

Little dreamt Ananias and Saphira when they lied to the Apostles that they should fall down dead at the Apostle's feet (Acts 5:5-10).

When we like Adam are cast into a deep sleep, a thousand to one, we lose a rib for it. Let me add that this security makes us worse than beasts. He that wants shame is like a beast; but he that lacks fear is worse than a beast. Bernard says, "Load an ass he cares not, because he was born to bear; but if you would force him upon the sire, or into a pit, he gives back with all his might, because he fears death." What a shame it is for men to cast themselves without fear into the jaws of destruction! When Balaam and his ass saw the Angel with a drawn sword in the way, he turned aside, his master could not force him on (Num. 22:23). We shall show ourselves more brutish than that ass if we precipitate ourselves into those ways wherein God stands with a drawn sword, eternally to destroy us.

No (to drive this to a head, and to lay the axe to the root of the tree), if we are secure and fearless, we shall prove ourselves and our kind to be worse than the devil himself. For St. James says of them, that "they believe and tremble," (James 2:19). They believe God's threats and tremble at his wrath.

In a word, as it is a misery that death should be to a man the first symptom of his sickness, so that man is to be bewailed with tears of blood who does not awaken until he is in hell, when it is too late.

All these considerations laid together, and well weighed, cannot eradicate this poisonous root of carnal security that is so diametrically and irreconcilably opposite to the fear of God. We will not (like the Israelites) sit down to "eat and drink, and rise up to play," (Exod. 32:6). But fear and care will be a more frequent guest in our breasts.

CHAPTER 12

Of audacious presumption in sinning, and the antidote against it.

A second sin that is contrary to the fear of God is presumptuous audaciousness, or an audacious presumption in sinning. It differs from security only in degree, for security is only a privation of fear, but presumption is joined with an accession of boldness. Indeed it is security strained to the highest peg, and dipped in a scarlet dye. The heathen use to call it a boldness like that of the giants spoken of by Ovid; A generation that despised God, and heaped mountain upon mountain, Pelion upon Ossa, and Olympus upon Pelion, as if they would dethrone God himself. Such are all those that harbor blasphemous thoughts, or such as belch out blasphemous words, that reflect upon God either directly, or by consequence; and those that in their actions pass the bounds of all modesty, like that unjust judge that "feared not God, neither regarded man," (Luke 18:2).

1. There is an audacious presumption in the thoughts. "The fool hath said in his heart there is no God," (Psa. 14:1). "Thou thoughtest that I was altogether such an one as thyself," (Psa. 50:21). As if he should say, "You imagine that I am a favorer of thievery, adultery, and slandering." And the

spectator of all hearts knows that our breasts are daily stiff, an anvil in which are forged, on which are framed many horrid thoughts of God, his worship, his servants. Such thoughts as we do not dare to utter. So that we had need to pray, that the thoughts of our hearts may be forgiven us, as Saint Peter counseled Simon Magus (Acts. 8:22). But in this we must leave men to stand or fall to their own masters.

2. There is an audacious presumption in words, when the poison of asps is under men's lips (Rom. 3:13). When men bid God battle, and stand in defiance against him. And that is *done,*

1. By that which we strictly call blasphemy, when men's tongues do not only walk through the earth, but they also set their mouths against the heavens, as David speaks (Psa. 73:9). Such was Lamech, saying to his wives in a bravery, "I have slain a...young man to my hurt. If Cain shall be avenged sevenfold, Truly Lamech seventy and sevenfold," (Gen. 4:23, 24). As if he should say, "I will slay the best man that shall but never so little offend me. And if God punishes Cain seven times, I will be revenged seventy seven times upon him that but razes my skin." He would be more severe than an enraged God. Such was Pharaoh who says, "Who is the Lord, that I should obey his voice to let Israel go? I know not the Lord, neither will I let Israel go," (Exod. 5:2). As if he should say, "I

know no Lord greater than myself. Such was Sennacherib, the Assyrian King, who sent this message to good King Hezekiah, "Let not thy God in whom thou trusteth deceive thee, saying, Jerusalem shall not be delivered into my hand," (2 Kings 19:10, 11). Which words Hezekiah calls, "A reproaching of the living God," (2 Kings 19:16). Such were those that in Job 21:14-15 said to God, "Depart from us; for we desire not the knowledge of thy ways. What is the Almighty, that we should serve him?" And those that said, "With our tongue we will prevail: our lips are our own: who is Lord over us," (Psa. 12:4). "Your words have been stout against me, saith the Lord...Ye have said, It is vain to serve God," (Mal. 3:13-14). And I have read of a king, who having received a strange blow from heaven, vowed he would be revenged upon God, and therefore gave strict commandment that for ten years no man should speak to God, or of God. And many of the Popes and Papalins have not fallen much short of those monsters of men, if some of their own authors say true. The time would fail me, should I reckon to you their numerous blasphemies that no truly Christian ear can handle. Leo X called the gospel a "Fable of Christ." And one of his slaves said that without the testimony of the Church, the Scriptures are no more authentic than Aesop's fables. Another says that if the Pope should carry troops of souls with him to hell, no man should dare to say to him, "Sir, why do you so?" Another says that there is well near as much virtue in Mary the mother's milk as in the Son's blood. Another at the Council of Trent called the cup in the Lord's Supper a cup of poison. What is this, but to affront, to confront, to dare God, to challenge him? And there are but too many loose Protestants that give their tongues to strange liberty to write with hostility against God, and all godliness. Black mouths, tongues set on fire of hell, such as dare say religion is but a devise to keep men in awe. Preaching is but prating. A religious life is but a malcontented life. He that uses plain dealing shall die a beggar, a young saint, an old devil. The heavens blush to see such foam to come forth from Christian men's mouths.

2. There is a presumption in words that displays itself in justifying and defending of sin, calling evil good, and good evil, light darkness, and darkness light, sweet bitter, and bitter sweet, as the Prophet speaks (Isa. 5:20). He enters the lists, and fights with God hand to hand, who defends what God hates. In this Jonah forgot much of himself, when God said to him, "Doest thou well to be angry?" And he said, "I do well to be angry, even unto death," (Jon. 4:9). This is to provoke "the Holy One of Israel to" anger as Isaiah speaks (Isa. 1:4).

3. It is the highest degree of presumption to boast of sin. None but brazen brows can do that (Isa. 48:4). He that is shameless is fearless. It is wrong enough to God to worship an idol. But David says, "Counfounded be all they that...boast themselves of idols," (Psa. 97:7). If a man may boast of his sins, then let the prisoner glory in his fetters, the dog in his vomit, and the infected person in his plague sore.

This is presumption in language.

3. There is presumption in *action*,

1. When a man dishonors God in that place wherein God uses, and ought to be worshiped; namely, the Temple. This is to abuse God to his face, and in his own house (Hos. 7:2).

2. When a man willfully dishonors God in a time of general humiliation, when others are bewailing their sins before God.

3. When a man sets himself as in the presence of God and yet then dissembles with his lips. As those (that with Saint Augustine before his conversion) pray against lust, and yet secretly wish that God would not hear their prayer. And all that with spleenful spirits come to the communion, professing before God that they are reconciled to their brethren when they intend no such thing. And those preachers that willingly deliver unsound doctrine to the

people, only to corrupt them, using the Name of God to poison their hearers, doing what in them lies to make God a liar. In a word, knights of the post with their hackney consciences that dare in a false oath call down God to testify to an untruth, which is so horrid a crime that I am persuaded that many a man now damned in hell would have been ashamed to be guilty of.

4. When a man therefore breaks a commandment merely because it is a command. As St. Augustine confessed that in his youth he robbed an orchard, not because he wanted apples, for he had as good or better at home, but only because he coveted what was forbidden.

5. When therefore a man abuses God more, because God is patient and longsuffering. Which sordidness of human disposition Solomon takes notice of and brands. He says, "Because sentence against an evil work is not executed speedily, therefore the heart of the sons of men is fully set in them to do evil," (Eccl. 8:11). This is to fight against God with his own weapon. To turn his grace into wantonness.

6. When man runs into a known gross sin that God's watchmen, his ministers have newly warned him of, or then when the Holy Spirit of God suggests motions to him to the contrary. This is to quench the spirit and despise prophesying

(1 Thess. 5:19, 20), to resist the Holy Spirit (Acts 7:51, 1 Thess. 4:8) and his instruments.

Lastly, when a man the more revolts from God, the more he is smitten, as they say in Isaiah 1:5. Like Pharaoh, whose heart was the more hardened, the sorer the plagues God inflicted on him. Like the Thracians that then shoot arrows against heaven, when it thunders and lightning strikes. Like Augustus, who having been tempest-tossed at sea defined Neptune the Sea-God, and in the middle of his Circean sports, he caused his image to be pulled down, to be revenged of him. Like Xerxes, who scourged the sea and wrote a bill of defiance against the hill Athos, because they intercepted him in his expedition.

I think the very naming of these things should move us to abhor them. But to win more upon our affections, let us *consider,*

1. That this audacious presumption is a despising of God. He that fears not God, condemns him.[8] "Wherefore doth the wicked condemn God?" David says (Psa. 10:13). For a superior to despise his inferior is no wonder, but for a peasant to despise his prince; for a piece of clay, for a worm, to slight his maker is intolerable. "They that despise me shall be lightly esteemed," says God (1 Sam. 2:30).

---

[8] *Quod non inetuitur contemnitur.* Lactantius.

Saint Paul was grieved at the heart that by sins of infirmity he offended his God. He says, "The evil which I would not, I do...O wretched man that I am! who shall deliver me from the body of death?" (Rom. 7:19, 24). Shall he groan under infirmities and shall we make no conscience of presumptions? God forbid.

3. What do you mean, fond man, to wrestle thunderbolts out of the hand of God that would delight to pour blessings upon you? "Who hath hardened himself against God, and prospered," asks Job (Job 9:4). Sennacherib slighted God and the fruit of it was, an Angel in one night slew his army, consisting of one hundred and eighty five thousand men; and he himself returning home was slain by his own sons in the temple of his god (2 Kings 19).

Libanius, a Philosopher at Antioch, demanding a good Christian in scorn, how the carpenter's son (meaning Christ) busied himself? He answered him that he was making a coffin for him and, indeed, presently after, he died.

In the year of our Lord 510, one Olympisu, an Arian Bishop, in a bath at Carthage, blasphemed openly the holy Trinity and the words were scarce out of his mouth but lightning descended thrice from heaven, and at length consumed him.

Julian, the uncle of the Emperor Julian, coming into a Christian Church, relieved himself on the communion table and struck Euzoius for reproving him for it. But shortly after, his entrails rotted and he voided his excrements at his mouth, and died. And Felix, Julian's treasurer, that jeered at Christ under the name of Mary's son, vomited blood night and day, until he died (according to Theodoret). You will say we hope none of us shall ever run into these extremes. But yet let us know that every presumptuous sin against God binds us over to as great mischiefs as any I have named. Will we believe Saint Paul? He says, "For if we sin wilfully after that we have received the knowledge of the truth, there remaineth no more sacrifice for sins, But a certain fearful looking for of judgment and fiery indignation," (Heb. 10:26, 27). The presumptuous are reserved to the Day of Judgment says Saint Peter (2 Pet. 2:9, 10). The arrows you shoot against heaven shall fall back on your own head again. "Woe to him," says the Prophet, "that striveth with his Maker! Let the potsherd strive with the potsherds of the earth," (Isa. 45:9). What do the waves gain by striking against a rock? They do not stir them, but dash themselves in pieces. "It is hard for thee to kick against the pricks," says our Savior to Saul (Acts 9:5). If you "will walk contrary unto me," says God, "Then will I also walk contrary unto you," (Lev. 26:23, 24). O! then let that of David be our prayer, "Keep back thy servant from presumptuous sins; let them not have dominion over me: then shall I be upright, and I shall be innocent from the great transgression," (Psa. 19:13).

This presumption is a second vice contrary to the fear of God. And therefore Solomon opposes hardening of the neck to fear (Pro. 28:14). And Aristotle says that those that are fearless, they slight God and man: they are audacious and presumptuous. This is the Goliath that bids defiance to God.

CHAPTER 13

Of superstitious fear, and the counter poison against it.

A third sin that is opposite to the true fear of God is superstition. Fear, when mean fear where no fear is (Psa. 53:3), as the Psalmist speaks. That is, where no true ground of fear is. And this may *be*,

1. When men fear to do that which God permits and allows to be done. So the Jews feared to name the name Jehovah. They thought the high Priest only might name it, and that but once in the year, and only in the Holy of Holies. Such were the Christians newly converted. They yet scrupulously observed days and abstained from meats, as upon the immediate tie of conscience from God. Such are some Romans also, that fear more to eat an egg at some set times, than they fear to swear or curse, or drink drunk. Again, they fear to allow marriage to Priests, which God allows. Paul says, "Have we not power to lead about a sister, a wife, as well as other apostles?" (1 Cor. 9:5) of which Saint Peter was one. "Marriage is honourable in all," says the Apostle (Heb. 13:4). This is a superstitious fear, to dread that as unlawful which God has left as indifferent, which me may do, or not do.

2. When men fear to do that, that God does indeed indispensably command. As the church of Rome fears to suffer the laity to read the Scripture in a known tongue, when Christ

has strictly enjoined the searching of the Scriptures on all (John 5:39). And they fear on the pretense of many ridiculous consequences to grant to the laity the cup in the Eucharist, though by the denial of it they prove themselves enemies to the primitive institution of the Sacrament, as St. Paul relates in (1 Cor. 11:23-25). So the Anabaptists fear to take an oath before a magistrate when an oath lawfully taken is a part of God's worship. Jeremiah says, "Thou shalt swear, The Lord liveth," (Jer. 4:2). That is, on warrantable occasion. God says, "If they will diligently learn the ways of my people, to swear by my name...They shall be built in the midst of my people," (Jer. 12:16), for "an oath for confirmation is to them an end of all strife," (Heb. 6:16). Again the Anabaptists fear to wage war for any cause whatsoever, when indeed there is a curse denounced against them that will not help the Lord against the mighty. It is one thing to say "help the Lord against the mighty," but entirely different when you place an *of* in between *help* and *the*. They will say that was under the Law. But what can they answer then to our Savior's words, "He that hath no sword, let him sell his garment and buy one," (Luke 22:36)?

3. When men fear to omit that which God nowhere commands, as the Romanists do too often. Of which their superstitions God may justly say as he did of the Israelites, "I

commanded them not, neither came it into my mind," (Jer. 32:35).

4. When mean fear to omit that which God forbids, as Papists fear to ores-slip the adoration of a saint, or of an angel, against which adoration God's jealousy smokes. "Thou shalt worship the Lord thy God, and him only shalt thou serve," Christ says (Matt. 4:10).

In a word, there is a superstitious fear when men are troubled at the crossing of the hare, the falling of the salt toward them, and the stumbling at the threshold. They think these things are in some way actionable, such as when men are daunted at the conjunctions of the planets and other stars in their several houses. These vanities, God dissuades his people from as heathenish, and not becoming the servants of God. "Thus saith the Lord, Learn not the way of the heathen, and be not dismayed at the signs of heaven; for the heathen are dismayed at them. For the customs of the people are vain," (Jer. 10:2-3). These foolish fears and the true fear of God cannot stand together. "For in the multitude of dreams and many words there are also diverse vanities: but fear thou God," Solomon says (Eccl. 5:7).

These are the several kinds of superstitious fears, though those that are guilty of some of these kinds of fear shall rise up in judgment against many of us. As they that think it unlawful to swear at all shall condemn those that stuff their common speech with oaths, and those that forswear themselves. And they that think it unlawful to war or go to suit at all shall condemn those that thirst after blood; and like salamanders love to live in the flame of contention. Yet we must be dissuaded from this scrupulous fear.

1. Because it argues a weakness in our judgment when we do not know the bounds and precincts of our Christian liberty (when we do not know what we may do, what we must do, what we need not to do, what we ought not to do, what is necessary, what is unlawful, what is indifferent). And therefore St. Paul calls one who makes everything out to be scandalous "weak in the faith," (Rom. 14:1).

2. To frame to ourselves doubts and scruples where God makes none is both to do what is thankless and what is hateful. It is thankless, for God will say to us as to them in Isaiah 1:12, "Who hath required this at your hand?" No, it is hateful. It is hateful to good men. "I have hated them that regard lying vanities," (Psa. 31:6). It is hateful to God. "They have chosen their own ways," says God, "I...will bring their fears upon them; because...they chose that in which I delighted not." We know that with us nothing is more nauseous or tedious than that man who, upon an ignorant fear to offend us, leave undone that which we would willingly

have done or importunately fastens that on us which we count a trouble.

CHAPTER 14

Of the servile fear of God.

A fourth sin contrary to the true fear of God is the servile or slavish fear of God: When men fear him only for that treasury of wrath which he has in his hand and can at his pleasure pour in full vials upon us, both in this life and eternally. This was King Abimelech the pagan's fear. This was Balaam the witch's fear. This was Judas the traitor's fear, which we are to be dissuaded from.

1. Because it moves a man to run from God, who is the fountain of all our good, as a slave would run from his master, or as a felon would break out of prison, that he might never see the face of his judge.

2. Because it works in man a hatred of God so that he often wishes that there were no God, or that God were blind, that he might not be an eyewitness of his wickedness, or that he were impotent, unable to punish him for his rebellion. It is as true of a servile fearer of God as it was of Saul, that the more he feared David, the more he became his enemy (1 Sam. 18:29).

3. Because it makes a man a hypocrite. It suffers him only to avoid those sins that are of the grossest bulk, that do lay waste the conscience. It moves him only to forbear, but not mortify his sin.

Lastly, this servile fear is but an earnest of hell torments in many a wretched soul.

They that consider this will grant me that such a fear as this is to be crucified with the rest of the body of sin. Not that it is unlawful to fear God for his judgments, but to fear him for his judgments only. That is upon no other nor better ground. I do not plead that this fear should be wholly abolished, but that it may be rectified and perfected, otherwise it is the daughter of infidelity, the sister of hatred, and the mother of despair.

CHAPTER 15

Of the excessive fear of the creature.

A fifth sin that fights against the kindly fear of God is the excessive fear of the creature. This is where man fears man, or any other creature either equally with, or more than God. And this we are dissuaded from.

1. Because as the throne and the bed can brook no rivals, neither can God endure that the fear due to him should be given to another. Hear how zealously he states the case, "Who art thou, that thou shouldest be afraid of a man that shall die, and of the son of man which shall be made as grass; And forgettest the Lord thy maker, that hath stretched forth the heavens, and laid the foundations of the earth?" (Isa. 51:12-13). And again, "Of whom hast thou been afraid or feared, that thou hast...not remembered me...and thou fearest me not?" (Isa. 57:11). Indeed this idolatry and sacrilege, to prefer the creature before the creator.

2. This over-fearing of man is a floodgate that lets in much mischief. It made Abraham deny his wife Sarah (Gen. 20:1). It made Jonah, when he was sent to Nineveh, to fly to Tarshish (Jon. 1:2-3). It made St. Peter to deny his master with an oath and a bitter execration. Have we not need then to deny this fear?

3. It is a ridiculous, brainless, reasonless thing to fear man more than God. We use to laugh at children that fear armor more than the man who wears it. Saint Austin imputes it to man's extreme folly. Men fear the prison, but they do not fear hell. They fear temporal torment, but they do not fear the pains of unquenchable fire. They fear the first, but not the second death. An early father says, "Despite man his power by dreading a more supreme power." And again he says, "God commands one thing, the emperor another. What must a man's answer be? Pardon me, dreadful sir, you threaten prison, and God threatens hell." And again Augustine says, "What can man do? He can but sharpen his razor to saw off our hair, our heads are not in his power." Every good man may answer the proud menaces of men as Christ answered Pilate. Pilate said, "Knowest thou not that I have power to crucify thee?" to which Christ answered, "Thou couldest have no power at all against me, except it were given thee from above," (John 19:10, 11). Now who would fear a sword that is in the hand of him that loves him? Who would fear a slave or scullion more than the Lord, and his master? We would hiss at that man who should fear an under-officer having a royal protection from his king.

4. He that for the fear of man injures his God, many times loses God and man both, and is secured neither way. I

have read that a remorseless wretch, having his enemy at an advantage, held his pistol at breast and with him, if he loved his life, to renounce his God. To save his life, he did so, whereupon he shot him saying this, "Now my revenge is perfect, both upon my body and your soul." We see how little the fear of man will advantage us. For in this sense, he that would save his life, may chance to lose it, as our Savior admonishes (John 12:25).

Lastly, God will pay us home in our own coin if we will fear men more than we ought, we shall fear men more than we would. The sound of an aspen leaf may chase us, we shall fly when no man pursues us (Lev. 26:36, Prov. 28:1). As the Burgundians feared that all the reeds they saw were lances. Certainly he deserves to fear all things who does not fear God above all. Where the true fear of one would acquit us from the fear of many.

CHAPTER 16

A serious exhortation to the fear of God, and first of the manner, how we ought to fear him.

What is past is dissuaded, what is next shall be commended. Now that I have untaught the false fears, I must have leave to teach the true fear of God. Every plant that God has not planted must be rooted up and the true bred fear of God must be implanted in our hearts. And there are not more pathetical moving, zealous, frequent counsels, commands, exhortations to any theological virtue, to any grace, than to this royal grace of the fear of God. It is God's wish. "O that there were such an heart in them, that they would fear me!" (Deut. 5:29, 6:1-2, 13, 24). It is his commandment three times imposed in one chapter. The book of Deuteronomy is full of this theme, "And now, Israel, what doth the Lord thy God require of thee, but to fear the Lord thy God," (Deut. 10:12). And in this Deuteronomy is a right Deuteronomy, repeating this law the second time, (for so the *word* imports) no again; and again almost in every chapter, certainly there is much in it, else there needed not such double iterations, and inculcations. This was a lesson that would vouchsafe to teach from heaven, and he required that parents should instill it into their children (Deut. 4:10). Our Savior divided the Old

Testament into Moses, the Psalms, and the Prophets (Luke 24:44). And all these books often and seriously commend the fear of God to us. We have heard Moses, now for the Psalms: "Let all the earth fear the Lord: let all the inhabitants of the world stand in awe of him," (Psa. 33:8). "O fear the Lord, ye his saints," (Psa. 34:9). For the Prophets: "Let the Lord God of hosts be your fear," (Isa. 8:13). In the New Testament: "Work out your own salvation with fear and trembling," says Saint Paul (Phil. 2:12). "Fear God, honour the king," says St. Peter (1 Pet. 2:17). We see that the fear of God is not out of date under the gospel. The glad tidings of great things do not exclude holy fear.

Neither are ignoble, poor men only obliged to fear God, but also the greatest person, or the sun, looks on. Princes are gods before men, but they are but men before God (Psa. 82:6-7). There inferiors fear them, and they must fear God. This fear is imposed upon rulers, "The God of Israel said, the Rock of Israel spake to me, He that ruleth over men must be just, ruling in the fear of God," (2 Sam. 23:3). On judges, Jehoshaphat said to the judges, "Take heed what ye do: for ye judge not for man, but for the Lord, who is with you in the judgment. Wherefore now let the fear of the Lord be upon you," (2 Chr. 19:6, 7). There are many yokes that may press some shoulders, but not others, but no neck can withdraw itself from this yoke. And now let me do as that Priest did at Bethel. He taught them how they should fear the Lord (2 Kings 17:28). And indeed, a man has need to seek as for silver, and search as for hidden treasure, to understand the fear of the Lord, as Solomon says (Pro. 2:4, 5). I shall apply myself to the readers, as David does to the people, "Come, ye children, hearken unto me: I will teach you the fear of the Lord," (Psa. 34:11). To descend to particular: first, we must so fear God as to worship, honor, and reverence him in thought, in word, and in deed; especially in the use of his sacred ordinances. "Ye that fear the Lord, praise him; all ye the seed of Jacob, glorify him; and fear him, all ye the seed of Israel," (Psa. 22:23). We see fear and praise, fear and glorifying of God, must go hand in hand together. And again, "Give unto the Lord the glory due unto his name: bring an offering, and come into his courts. O worship the Lord in the beauty of holiness: fear before him, all the earth," (Psa. 96:8-9). Again, an angel said with a loud voice, "Fear God, and give glory to him...and worship him," (Rev. 14:7). He that does not fear God, cannot worship him, and he that does not worships God, does not fear him (*Quod non metuitur, non colitur*).

2. We may and ought to fear God for his threatenings and for his punishments. "I am afraid of thy judgments," David says (Psa. 119:120). If the lion roars, who will not fear, and if

God threatens, who can but fear (Amos 3:8)? When God threatened a universal flood, Noah was moved with fear (Heb. 11:7). And when God threatened such a hail should fall in Egypt that should kill every man and beast in the field, the text says, "He that feared the word of the Lord...made his servants and cattle flee into the houses," (Exod. 9:20). Nature will tutor us to fear thus. But we must also fear when the judgments of God are executed on others, though as yet they do not press us; as an ingenuous child trembles when he sees his father strike a servant, though he is not angry with him. "Thou puttest away all the wicked of the earth like dross...My flesh trembleth for fear of thee," David says (Psa. 119:119, 120). And when God smote Uzzah to death it is said that David "was afraid of the Lord that day," (2 Sam. 6:6, 9). And when Ananias and Saphira for lying fell down dead at the Apostle's feet, the text says in one place that "great fear came on all them that heard these things," (Acts 5:5). And in another place, "fear came upon all the church, and upon as many as heard these things," (Acts 5:11) though they were not guilty of the same sin that was their bane. When a neighbor's house is on fire, no man is senseless as not to fear his own house.

3. We must fear God, not only for his judgments, but also for his mercy, as a chaste wife fears a loving husband from who she expects not a harsh word, much less a blow. "God

will not afflict. Men do therefore fear him," says Job (Job 37:23-24). We ought to fear God both because he afflicts and because he does not afflict. We must fear him for his justice and severity, and for his goodness. "They shall fear the Lord and his goodness in the latter days," says the Prophet (Hos. 3:5). Therefore, God calls his people a revolting, a rebellious people, because they did not say in their heart, "Let us now fear the Lord our God, that giveth rain, both the former and the latter, in his season: he reserveth unto us the appointed weeks of the harvest," (Jer. 5:24). Which plainly shows that we must fear God for giving seasonable, as well as unseasonable weather, as we must love a just as well as a merciful God. So we must fear a merciful as well as a just God.

That is (in the fourth place) we must be scarce to offend and dishonor that God who is so abundantly merciful to us. The fear of God and the discarding of sin must go together. "Stand in awe, and sin not," David says. "All the people shall hear, and fear, and do no more presumptuously," says Moses (Deut. 17:13). And again, "Those that remain shall hear, and fear, and shall henceforth commit no more any such evil among you," (Deut. 19:20). Nehemiah says to the nobles, "It is not good that ye do: ought ye not to walk in the fear of our God?" "Fear the Lord, and depart from evil," says Solomon. It is a plain mocking of God to say we fear him and yet not fear minutely to perpetrate that which is derogatory and odious to him. Like those that fear the Lord forsook, and yet served their graven images (2 Kings 17:41).

5. Fear of God must be accompanied and seconded with obedience to God. "That thou mightest fear the Lord thy God, to keep all his statutes," in Deuteronomy 6:2, 13. "Serve the Lord with fear," says the psalmist. "Fear the Lord, and serve him," says Samuel (1 Sam. 12:24). We know that service does not stand in receiving wages, in eating and drinking, in making legs, and wearing liveries, but in obedience. Neither does the service of God consist in outside complement, or in-wearing the badge of Christianity, but in the works of obedience to our heavenly Lord and master. We must so fear God as neither to make God to serve us by our sins (Isa. 43:24), yet not to serve ourselves on God, but both in doing and in suffering, to resign ourselves to God's will and pleasure.

6. We must so fear God as to cleave to him and not to run from him; as to love him and not to hate him; as to trust in him, and not to distrust him. We must serve God with fear and we must serve God without fear, that is without distracting and dissident fear, says Zacharias (Luke 1:74). Saint Bernard says that it is a sorrowful and a profitless fear that therefore does not obtain pardon, because it fears to seek

pardon. Fear and love, fear and faith, and confidence must be inseparably united.

7. We must so fear God in, and through, and for God's sake, to fear those whom God has as his substitutes set over us. Subjects must fear their sovereign, and God in him. "Fear God, honour the king," says Peter (1 Pet. 2:17). Children must fear their parents, "Ye shall fear every man his mother, and father," says Moses (Lev. 19:3), God in their parents, and their parents, in and for God.

First God, and then their parents. Wives must fear and reverence their husbands. "Let the wife see that she reverence her husband," Saint Paul says (Eph. 5:33). Servants must fear their masters. "Servants, be obedient to them that are your masters according to the flesh, with fear and trembling," says Paul (Eph. 6:5), who elsewhere conjoins obedience to masters with fear of God. "Servants, obey in all things your masters according to the flesh; not with eye-service...but in singleness of heart, fearing God," (Col. 3:22). That is, fearing God in their masters, and their masters for God's sake.

8. We must fear God above all the creatures in the world, though all their force and vigor were united together. This is the meaning of that of our Savior, "Fear not them which kill the body, but are not able to kill the soul: but rather fear him which is able to destroy both soul and body in

hell," (Matt. 10:28). Do not fear him that can kill the body, that is fear not him so much as God. Shall we fear the creature and not God for whose sake only we fear the creature. For what strength has any creature where with God invests it not? What can any creature do for you, or against you, that God cannot do? What can any man do against or for you that God does not permit, and that he cannot interrupt, or revoke? The strength of all creatures combined together is but infirmity, weakness to God's power; human policy is folly to God's wisdom. We fear a giant more than an infant, a mountain more than a molehill, a flame than a spark, a sea, then a drop; why then do we not fear God more than all things?

Lastly, we must fear God always, constantly, without intermission, or interruption. In youth, in age, in adversity, in prosperity. "That ye might fear the Lord your God for ever," says Joshua (Jos. 4:24). "But I thy servant fear the Lord from my youth," says Obadiah (1 Kings 18:12). "They shall fear thee as long as the sun and moon endure," David says (Psa. 72:5). "Be thou in the fear of the Lord all the day long," Solomon says (Pro. 23:17). There are many duties that are sometimes out of season, but the fear of the Lord is never out of season.

So, I have displayed before the reader's eye the manner how we ought to manage our fear of God. In which I have studied plainness to leave the lowest capacities without excuse. In matter of direction in a duty, in which depends life, or death, it is absurd to walk in clouds; or to use the enticing words of man's wisdom.

CHAPTER 17

The means by which the fear of God may be wrought

and increased.

Next to the manner of how we ought to fear God, the means by which this fear is ordinarily ingenerated and confirmed and increased come next to hand.

1. Be a companion of all those that fear God, as David professes that he was (Psa. 119:63). The company of bold, foolhardy wretches that dare venture into any sin is the next way to make you, whoever you are, fearless and careless, until sudden and unrecouperable mischief falls upon you.

2. The hourly consideration of God's all-seeing eye will keep the fear of God lively and fresh in the heart. That man cannot but be fearful and careful that thinks within himself that he lives always in the eyes of such a Judge, that is the great and unswayed spectator of all things.

3. Read and hear the word of God frequently and diligently. There, O Christian, will you find what God is, and what the fear of God is, and what unanswerable reasons you have to fear him. "Gather me the people together, and I will make them hear my words, that they may learn to fear me," (Deut. 4:10). "And all the people shall hear, and fear," says Moses (Deut. 17:13). And again, "that their children...may hear,

and learn to fear the Lord," (Deut. 31:13). The soul is in the ear, what do you know but that upon your constant attendance on this sacred ordinance, God may strike the speeding blow and work his fear in you?

Lastly, we must daily and zealously pray to him, whom we ought to fear, to implant this fear in us. David will put words into our mouths, "Lord...unite my heart to fear thy name," (Psa. 86:11). Arouse our drowsy, leaden, and secure spirits, and cause the spirit of your fear to rest upon us, that at all times, in all places, above all things, we may fear you.

Much more might be added, but he who conscionably uses these means cannot be a stranger to the fear of God. You will say, "These means are but ordinary and plain." All the better! What wise physician will try a chemical, curious way to cure a patient, when the known remedies will do the deed? That is only to try conclusions on the patient. We use to say, plain iron may do that, which gold cannot do. You cannot now say the way is dark, for you have had sufficient direction; nor, that the well is deep, and you have no bucket to draw with, for wholesome means have been prescribed. If we now do not fear God, it is because we will not. The next work, then, must be to bow our perverse wills and to provoke our cold, dull affections to this transcendent grace.

CHAPTER 18

Arguments for and motives unto the fear of God.

And now what incentives shall I use to work our affections to this fear? Let us look on God's little book, his word, and on his great book of nature, the world; and there is no line in the one, nor thing in the other, but argues hard, and powerfully pleads for the fear of God. But not to let my discourse loose into a hedgeless field, let us *remember,*

1. The surpassing excellency of this grace in itself. It is an epitome, and abstract of all religion. That which Moses calls "fear" (Deut. 6:13), our Savior quoting that place calls "worship," (Matt. 4:10). And in the Greek, the same words signify fear and religion, as if all religion lay in this fear. As a tradesman commonly takes his name from that in which he most deals, so fear and religion go together. Obadiah "feared God greatly," (1 Kings 18:3). And of Hanani, "feared God above man," (Neh. 7:2). And of Job, "He feared God," (Job 1:1). No, the fear of God is the *Alpha and Omega*, the beginning and the end, the complement, and perfection of all. Solomon calls it, "the beginning of wisdom," (Prov. 1:7) and the conclusion of all, (Eccl. 12:13). It is the root of wisdom. It is pertaining to the body, the *crown* of wisdom. I had need of the tongue of men and angels to give it its due praise and full character, *but,*

2. Let us turn our eyes upon God, the object of this fear, and we will find that he deserves, and may challenge our fear. And when we speak of God, we will with David give him this addition, God who "ought to be feared," (Psa. 76:11), *For,*

1. He is omnipotent and omniscient. "The eyes of the Lord are in every place, beholding the evil and the good," (Pro. 15:3). Therefore in every place stand in awe of him.

If a man were sure that his prince's eye was always on him, how fearful, how wary would he be in all his actions? Augustine says, "Fear him whose constant care is to look upon thee, and walk chastely; or if thou wilt needs offend, seek some retired place wherein God cannot see thee and do thy pleasure." What height of atheism is it to fear the eye of a child, and not to fear God's all-seeing eye?

2. He is omnipotent, "able to save and to destroy," says James (Jam. 4:12). Now power is the proper object of fear. "Thou, even thou, art to be feared: and who may stand in thy sight when once thou art angry?" David says (Psa. 76:7). And therefore God might well with indignation ask the question, "Fear ye not me? saith the Lord: will ye not tremble at my presence, which have placed the sand for the bound of the sea by a perpetual decree, that it cannot pass it: and though the waves thereof toss themselves, yet can they not prevail; though they roar, yet can they not pass over it?" Our lives, our

souls are in God's hands. He has the keys to death and hell. "Thou turnest man to destruction," David says (Psa. 90:3). He is able to cast both body and soul into hell and shall we not fear him (Matt. 10:28)? Our Savior redoubles his words, "Fear him...yea, I say unto you, Fear him" (Luke 12:5) before whom man is but as a moth, as the dust of the balance.

3. God is as just, as jealous, as severe as powerful. He will not spare his own children the apples of his eye, the signets on his right hand, if they willfully offend him. "You only have I known of all the families of the earth: therefore I will punish you for all your iniquities," God says (Amos 3:2). No, he would not spare his only son when he would stand in the place of sinners. Now what guilty man does not fear an austere, upright, unswayed judge? What child does not fear an angry father? What servant does not fear his incensed master? Do you know what God's anger is? The fire kindled in his wrath burns to the lowest hell (Deut. 32:22) as God says, "when his wrath is kindled but a little. Blessed are they that put their trust in him," David says (Psa. 2:12). "Do they provoke me to anger?" says the Lord, "Do they not provoke themselves to the confusion of their own faces?" (Jer. 7:19). "It is a fearful thing to fall into the hands of the living God," says Saint Paul (Heb. 10:31). "Serve God acceptably with reverence and godly fear: For our God is a consuming fire," says the same

apostle (Heb. 12:28, 29). "Who among us shall dwell with everlasting burnings?" says the prophet (Isa. 33:14).

4. God is gracious, therefore fear him. "There is forgiveness with thee, that thou mayest be feared," the Psalmist says (Psa. 130:4). A loving wife is fearful to offend an indulgent husband. An obedient child is fearful to offend a careful father. And shall we turn God's grace into wantonness, and slight him for his kindness? That would be pitiful.

5. "There is none holy as the Lord," says Hannah (1 Sam. 2:2), therefore we ought to fear and reverence him. King Herod feared John Baptist because "he was a just and an holy man, and observed him," says the text (Mark 6:20). Shall a wicked man fear a man who is holy only by participation and shall we not fear God whose essence is holiness in itself? It is David's argument that we should worship, reverence God, "for he is holy," (Psa. 99:5).

6. Whatever God is in himself, we are sure he is our God, our Lord, our master, our Father. All which are strong obligations on us to fear him. "Sanctify the Lord of hosts...let him be your fear...and dread," (Isa. 8:13). There is one reason: He is God. But more than that he is our Lord, "If then I be a father, where is mine honour? and if I be a master, where is my fear?" says God (Mal. 1:6). He claims our fear by this undoubted right. It is Saint Peter's inference, "If ye call on the

Father...pass the time of your sojourning here in fear," (1 Pet. 1:17).

Lastly, if we do not regard the duty for its own sake, nor for God's sake, yet let us fear God for our own sake. For, (1.) The fear of God has temporal promises annexed to it. What do you desire? The fear of God will make you the owner of it. Would you have rest, and ease, and estate for yourself and yours? This fear brings it. David says, "What man is he that feareth the Lord?...His soul shall dwell at ease; and his seed shall inherit the earth," (Psa. 25:12, 13). Would you not be brought to poverty and penury? Then fear God. "There is no want to them that fear him," (Psa. 34:9). Would you live long? Why, "The fear of the Lord prolongeth days," says Solomon (Pro. 10:27). Would you have plentiful issue? It is promised to the fearers of God. Would you be content with your present estate (Psa. 128)? He that has the fear of the Lord "shall abide satisfied," says Solomon (Pro. 19:23). In a word, God counts nothing too dear for such. "By humility and the fear of the Lord are riches, and honour, and life," says Solomon (Pro. 22:4). Either you shall enjoy all these things, or that which is equivalent to them, or that which is better than them; or you shall be content with your present state. "Better is little with the fear of the Lord than great treasure," (Pro. 15:16). But (2.)

all this is but dross to the spiritual fruits of the fear of God. *For,*

1. It is the mother of wisdom (Pro. 1:7). "What man is he that feareth the Lord? Him shall he teach in the way that he shall choose...The secret of the Lord is with them that fear him: and he will shew them his covenant," (Psa. 25:12, 14). He that fears God shall be acquainted with the pith and marrow of God's will, when others shall scarce pierce the bark of it. This is true wisdom, to be wise to a man's self, as every fearer of God is (Pro. 9:12). "A prudent man foreseeth the evil, and hideth himself" under the wings of God's protection, so does every fearer of God (Pro. 27:12).

2. The fear of God is the porter of the soul that casts out sin, and keeps out sin; so Bernard says. It is the keeper of our innocence; so Cyprian says. It is the anchor of the soul that makes a man stable amidst all temptations; so Gregory says. "The fear of the Lord is clean," David says (Psa. 19:9), because it keeps men clean, as he that walks fearfully, and warily, walks surely, and cleanly. That way is safer the more suspicious we are of it. "By the fear of the Lord men depart from evil," says Solomon (Prov. 16:6). This was Joseph's curb, "How then can I do this great wickedness, and sin against God?" (Gen. 39:9).

3. The true fear of God expels all false fears, as Moses' rod did eat up all the Egyptian rods. It expels slavish fear because it is joined with joy. "Rejoice with trembling," David says (Psa. 2:11). This fear breeds eternal security. It expels the excessive fear of men. "Neither fear ye their fear...let God be your fear," says the Prophet (Isa. 8:12, 13). For indeed this fear is a counterpoison to that. "Though I walk through the valley of the shadow of death, I will fear no evil," David says (Psa. 23:4).

4. The fear of God is the mother of obedience. And therefore when David desired to walk in the true way, he desired that he might fear God, for no obedience without fear (Psa. 86:11). Everywhere in Scripture, fear and obedience are linked together. If we fear God, we will conscionably discharge all duties required in all our conditions, and relations (Eccl. 12:13; Deut. 5:29). Then judges would accept no persons and take no bribes (2 Chr. 19:5-7), then young men would honor their elders (Lev. 19:32). Then the wife would love, and obey the husband; children their parents, and servants their masters. Then executors would perform the will of the dead. And no man would offer to betray a trust. Then every state would be enjoined, and we should live godly and righteously, and peaceably, one by another. In a word, the fear of God is the nurse of perseverance unto the end. He that

is secure and presumptuous often falls off, when he that fears God and suspects himself, holds his ground. Fear breeds care, and care continuance. Had Peter feared more, he would not have fallen so foully. I do not speak of cowardly, but of faithful fear. It is God's promise in Jeremiah 32:40, "I will put my fear in their hearts, that they shall not depart from me."

Last of all, fear and godliness have the promises of the life to come (1 Tim. 4:8). The fear of God tends to life, says Solomon (Pro. 19:23). However the squares go now, I know it shall "go well with them that fear God," says the Preacher (Eccl. 8:12). And in Malachi 3:16, God writes a book of remembrance for them that fear him, and he promises that he will acknowledge them as his in the day when he shall make up his jewels.

Harder is that heart than the hardest adamant heart, with which all these arguments cannot prevail.

So I have given this point its due (as I conceive) yet wishing that an abler pen might add what I have omitted. My sack has corn in it to feed the hungry, though not gold in the mouth thereof to feed the humor of a fanciful reader. My aim is not to please the humorous, but to profit all. For censure, and detraction it will be lost on me, for I do not regard it. I do not pass man's judgment for "he that judgeth me is the Lord," (1 Cor. 4:4, Isa. 49:4). If I shall gain but one soul by this discourse I am abundantly paid, but though Israel is not gathered, yet my work is with my God.

FINIS

MAN'S DELINQUENCY

By William Price

[ORIGINAL TITLE PAGE]

Man's Delinquency
Attended by

DIVINE JUSTICE

Intermixed With

MERCY

Displayed in a Sermon to the Right
Honorable the House of LORDS
Assembled in Parliament, in the Abby Church
At Westminster, *November 25, 1646*
Being the Solemn Day of Their Monthly Fast.

By William Price, B.D. Pastor of *Waltam-Abby*;
And one of the Assembly of Divines.

Let not him blush to repent, who hath not blushed to commit
that that is to be repented of.

LONDON,
Printed by *R.R.* for *Richard Whitaker*, at the
Sign of the Kings Arms in St. *Paul's* Churchyard,
1646.

Die Veneis 26. Novembris 1646.

It is this day ordered by the LORDS in Parliament assembled, that this House gives thanks to Mr. Price, one of the Assembly of Divines, for his great pains taken in his *sermon* preached on the last *Fast Day* before the Lords of Parliament, in the Abby Church Westminster. And he is by this desired to print and publish the same; which is to be printed only by authority under his own hand.
John Brown. *Cleric. Parliament*

I appoint Richard Whitaker to print this Sermon.
William Price.

INTRODUCTORY LETTER

To the Right Honorable House of PEERS assembled in PARLIAMENT,

Right Honorable,

It was enough to impose that piece of penance on yourselves, to give this unpolished sermon its hearing; but it is much more that you should put your eye to further experience of patience. But since you are pleased to desire (which to me is a command) my hand against myself, by testifying my weaknesses in the exposing of this mean discourse to public view,

Answer. I obey. But then give him, whom you have so far emboldened, leave to mind you, that the Sermons your Lordships have heard, or should have heard, are to be reckoned in the inventories of your receipts from your God. To hear, and to read, is but contrary; you are also to bring forth; not only the leaves, of the good words, or resolutions; or fruit. Those of your sphere enter the lists of comparison with vines and olives, (Jud. 9:8-10), the choicest of trees in Jotham's parable. *And if a vine be fruitless, it is worthless, and will not yield a pin to hang a hat on,* (Ezek. 15:23). You are fixed in a higher orb, and attract all eyes to you. You, as a snail, or the Leviathan in the sea, leave a shining track and your example has a potent influence that stands on higher ground. As we say in arithmetic, in the first and lowest place is but one, in the second place 10, in the third 100; and so higher, and higher. And as the whitest ivory makes the blackest coal, the most generous wine the sharpest vinegar; as the shrewdest tempests come often out of the warmest corners, so the greatest injustice, and most unworthy demeanor we fear from Nobility and potency degenerated. Governors' actions are like Jeremiah's figs, or Origen's *Works*; if bad, *very* bad. Greatness disjoined from goodness is rather swelling, than a true, real magnitude. You are to give account at the great Audit-day, not only as Christians, but as Nobles, as Judges, as Senators, as Magistrates. It is good that you contemplated with a holy emulation the highest form of untainted *Religion*, unswayed with great integrity, uncorrupt in its justice, unconquerable with patience, with steady moderation, and surpassing temperance, that the sacred Scripture and other stories are growing more and more by your work.

When you read that *Manlins Torquatns* took off his own son's head for irregular running before a command, though his intents were fair, and his design successful, think to yourselves, that it is not fit to suffer your deputies to be eccentric, arbitrary, unlimited in their proceedings, where no *Order or Ordinance* of yours enables them. When you read that *Quintus Cincentus* was taken from the plough, and made *Dictator* of Rome, and when he had done his country the utmost service he conceived he could arrive to, he returned to his former meanness; such thoughts will quench soaring ambition in you. When you find that *Lucius Vaterius*, a Roman Consul, dying, having long held the custody of the Treasury of Rome, was yet so poor at his death, that the Commonwealth was pressed to defray the charges of his funeral, you will, like *Jethro's Justicers*, hate that ignoble dry drunkenness and covetousness, (Exod. 18:21). When you see it said of *Fabritius*, and testified by his enemy, that the sun could sooner be justled out of his orb, then he out of the *orb of justice*, you cannot but be dispassionate, un-prepossessed, unprejudiced Judges. Justice is painted with scales in her hand, not to weigh gold, but right. When a woman kneeled to Francis I of France for justice; *stand up* (he said) *woman, justice I owe you; if you beg anything, ask for mercy*. When you read that Alphonsus King of Arragon read over the Bible with commentaries fourteen times, you will study the Scripture more. O! do not let poor blind heathens, that had no better conduct then the glowworms twilight of divine nature, and unrenewed reason. Do not let blindfolded Papists cast you behind them, and rise in judgment against you. God expects that you should outweigh and outdo the most advanced moralists. Your helps heavenward are more and mightier than theirs, your light clearer, your obligations to God more, and greater. God has honored you above others, who are but of the same mold with others, as the ground of the rainbow is but a common exaltation, it is only the sun that gilds and enamels it with such various colors. Study as much as in you lies, to return honor to him from whom you had your honor, if you would not love your honor, or at least be lost by it. Epaminondas so carried his honor, that he seemed rather to contribute luster to, then to borrow it from his honor. It will be worthy of you to be a dignity to your dignity. An undeserving person honored, is but as a dwarf, set him on Olympus, he is but a dwarf *still.* A worthy person honored is a Colossus, *great,* though he may be in the bottom of a pit. Your honor is a talent with which God betrusts you, which if you embase, he that gave it can recall it. Dignity, like oil is airy, and slippery. Henry IV, the Emperor who fought two and fifty pitched battels, was compelled by poverty to petition for a prebends place at Spyre to maintain him in his old age. And Comminez says, that he saw the Duke of Excester, who married King Edward IV's sister, begging barefoot in the low-countries. But I forget myself; and should crave pardon, and Apologize for the length both of my sermon and dedication, but that would make me longer. May you live and die full of honor.

May you be instruments of God's glory here, and vessels of eternal glory hereafter, is, and shall be the prayer of Your Lordship's

Most humbly devoted servant in the Gospel,
Of Jesus Christ,
William Price

A SERMON BEFORE THE HOUSE OF LORDS ON THE LAST MONTHLY FAST-DAY

Ezra 9:6-8:

Verse 6. And I said, O my God, I am ashamed, and blush (*or, I am confounded and ashamed*) to lift up my face (*or my eyes*) unto thee, my God: for our iniquities are increased over our head, and our trespass is grown up unto the heavens, (*Diverse Translation*).

Verse 7. Since (*or, from*) the days of our fathers have we been in a great trespass even unto this day: And for our iniquities have we, our Kings, and our Priests been delivered into the hands of the Kings of the lands, to the sword, to captivity, and to the spoil, and to confusion of face, as it is (*or, appeareth*) this day.

Verse 8. And now for a little space (or, a moment) grace hath been showed from the Lord our God, to leave us (or, in causing) a remnant to escape; and to give (*or, in giving us*) a nail in his holy place, that our God may lighten our eyes, and give us a little reviving in our bondage (*or, servitude*).

This is a gloomy day of public humiliation and the argument of this chapter (on a branch of which my lot is now fallen) is drooping, and heaviness, (verse 5). The people indeed we find trembling (in the next chapter) for the immoderate reign, (chap. 10:9); for it seems the clouds then dispensed their treasures too fast, as now they do. But a dung-hilly worldling can howl on his bed under a loss or cross. But our Ezra mourns more for the blackness, then the burning of the coal *of sin*. A formalist may sometimes feel a legal fit, a pang of sorrow for his own sins: but Ezra laments the miscarriages of others; the people of Israel, the Priests, the Levites, the Princes and Rulers, who were all embarked in that delinquency that he deplores. Ezra's humiliation began within, but ended not there. His sorrow-pressed heart finds a vent in all the solemn dress, and equipage that grief uses to assume, and put on; laceration of garments, plucking the hair from his head, and beard, pensively sitting down with silence, stupefaction, astonishment until the evening. And lest his passion should be interpreted an emasculating, sullen stupidity, and amazed dullness, rather than an active repentance, (which ought to be a fruit-bearing tree, and not a dead log) he raises and rouses himself, and betakes himself to his knees, and spreads out his hands heavenward (the usual visible demonstrations of the height of devotion) and offers the fruit of his lips, pouring out his soul, clothing his sad apprehensions with airy, but solid and melting expressions, breathing forth his complaints to him who only could relieve him, in a prayer that here is memorized and conveyed to posterity, distilling from his own pen. It is recorded of him, that he was a prompt scribe. His tongue was as the pen of a ready writer when he commenced, and presented this suit at the throne of grace; and his pen is as a tongue to report it to succeeding generations as an exemplary model, or platform to steer us in putting up our petitions on emergent occasions. *"And I said, O my God, etc."* And so is the text allied to the context.

If you now please (Right Honorable, and the rest beloved in our Savior) to see how the words that lie before us shine with their own native substance, without borrowed luster. They are considerable under the notion of a prayer; an ordinance, that if duly managed, can open and shut heaven, bind and loosen the hands of the Omnipotent, blast designs, countermine mines, command, countermand men, tie up devils, throw Rome into Tiber. It demonstrates a duty that sanctifies fasting, as fasting quickens and imps the wings of it, (*Summe Epitomie*).

Here the prayer the Petitioner draws for himself and his people as with a black coal, verses 6-7. But draws his God with orient colors, verse 8, vilifying, nullifying man; or if any diminutive can be added below abasement itself. but magnifying God, (*Anatomis. Parts.*).

1. He decries himself and Israel, discovering his sorrow by the impression of his shame, and the expression of their National misery.

1.) The impression of his shame, verse 6. "O my God, I am confounded, *etc.*"

2.) The expression of his and Israel's misery, in a self-arraignment, and a self-condemnation.

1.] His self-arraignment appears in drawing up a large indictment made up of an ingenious confession, and an heightening aggravation.

(1.) A confession of their sin under the varied and reiterated language of "iniquities," and "trespasses"; emphatical and comprehensive titles.

2.) The aggravation of those transgressions, *By,*

1. The dimensions of them; height and depth. The continued quantity, the magnitude, "increased", multiplied.

2. The customary inveterateness, "From the days of our fathers to this day."

3. The Epidemicalness, and the spreading universality; the guilt of "Kings" and "Priests" is mentioned here, verse 7. And if we cast our eyes back to the first, and second verses, we shall find "Levites," "people" and "rulers" all put into this bill of attainder.

Yet he does not content himself with this self-arraignment; but erects a tribunal within his own breast, and there he passes an impartial judgment on himself, and the rest involved and engulfed in this blame. "For our iniquities have we been delivered up."

Delivered; To whom? To what?

1. To whom? To men; and one man is naturally a wolf to another; and those men potent, "Kings"; and those many; and they ethnics, heathenish, the "Kings of the nations."

2. To what delivered? "To sword, to captivity, to spoil, to confusion of face"; and that not imminent, but incumbent; not feared, but felt; all too apparent, "As it is (or appears) this day." So different translations have it.

2. Having in this way depressed man, he exalts God in his most magnetic, attractive, amiable attribute, "Grace"; amplified by the fruit growing on that root, "rescue, preservation; causing a remnant to escape". And "settlement; giving us a nail in his holy place." And these comfortable "ends" that God leveled at; the "lightning in their eyes, and reviving their hearts in their servitude."

This is the anatomy, these the lineaments of the text. Which by this time you may perceive, corresponds and may aptly entitle itself to the times, and the time; to this day, an audience, being composed of "rulers," and "people"; the parties

128

mentioned in this chapter. May the text prove as profitable, as it is *seasonable.*

Here is a large vintage; I cannot stand to pluck every grape; I must present them to you by clusters, and (like our geographers) set down a line for a River, and a spot for a whole Country; here being such an ocean, a continent of matter under my hands.

1. I take my point from Ezra's decrying, and vilifying himself, and Israel. And in this from the "impression" of his shame, "And I said, O my God, I am ashamed, and blush" (or as other Translations render it, "I am confounded, and ashamed") "to lift up mine eyes to thee, my God."

Both are agreeable to the Original, that uses two words, importing "shame, blushing, confusion of face," or "eyes," the seat of shame.

Shame is sometimes a vice, sometimes a punishment, sometimes a virtue. A vice, as Tacitus writes of Domitian's blushing, it was a shame, by which he fortified himself against shame. As Seneca faith of Sylla, "He was never more to be dreaded, then when he blushed." Sometimes shame is a punishment; as at the end of the seventh verse. But here in Ezra it is a *virtue*; a shame of which he did not need to be ashamed.

Shame has its source within, caused either by self-consciousness, when a guilty soul sweats with reflecting on itself. Or, from a piercing apprehension of others unworthiness, which was Ezra's motive in the text; he was ashamed, because Israel was not ashamed. This shame was not his accuser, but compurgator. He enters a caveat against them by the coloring of his cheek.

The badge of shame or modesty is blushing, the transfusion of a vermilion through the face, which when blood moves into the cheeks we call it *the color of virtue*. Though it is often an infirmity, yet often an index of ingenuity, as thistles show us that the ground is fertile while bearing them.

"Confusion" (which in some translations is inserted here) is the meridian, zenith, vertical point of shame, it can mount no higher, (margin); As shame tied up the peoples tongues when they were argued of halting between two opinions, they "answered not a word", (1 Kings 18:21); and Joshua's tongue when Israel was foiled at Ai, "What shall I say?" (Joshua 7:8) this is that confusion here spoken of; and this possesses Ezra too. "O my God," (he says) "I am confounded," at a stand, filled with astonishment, that Israel should so degenerate and degrade themselves. So planet-struck was he, that he could not, dared not lift up his eyes. His looks were demise, his eyes staked to the ground, as the Publicans, that "would not lift up so much as his eyes to heaven." (Luke18:13).

And yet this shame of Ezra does not deliver him over to despondency, or despair; for twice failing in a breath he speaks of God as his, "O my God, O my God." Adam's shame drove him from God, (Gen. 3:8, 10); Ezra's drives him to God. it fastens his hold, so that he applies God the closer to him, "O my God." Which commends this note to us; the pearl, the point lies above ground, *That,*

Observation 1. "They that are at odds with sin because it is sin, will blush even at other men's sins." Ezra did not share in this particular crime, that so fills his heart with grief, and his face with shame. As in the prophecies, the silver moon is said to be confounded, and the spotless sun to be ashamed,

(Isa. 24:23). And stars of the clearest beam, and first magnitude in the Church of God have been, and ought to be thus modest. "Your mother (God says) shall be sorely confounded, she that bare you shall be ashamed," (Jer. 50:12). A Christian's apostasy is said to put Christ to open shame, (Heb.6.6). Were he on earth, or now receptive of this passion, the sins of men would put him to it. But mere men have more reason to blush for men.

Reasons for this: Whether because sin is so shameful in its own nature, so that the Scripture makes it enter the wishes of comparison with the most sordid things that earth can show. Or, whether to acquit themselves from the guild of other men's sins, which we make our own by not being affected with them. Or, whether from others aberrations we are prompted to review our own natural leprous deformity, which we derived from our parents' loins, and unhappily improved and expressed, until God recalled us to himself. Or, we are minded, that the seeds of the most prodigious sins are in us; though grace restrain or mortify them. Else a Simon Peter might prove a Simon Magus; a Saint a Devil; every one of us a Saul, a Balaam, a Judas, a witch, a traitor to our Savior. These recoiling thoughts draw the color into our cheeks. Or, whether by command, counsel, connivance, or any other way, we have been accessory to others' falls, since in religion all accessories are principals. Or, whether it is that we consider, that the sacred name of God is blasphemed, and the reputation of religion blasted by black mouths, as if it were but an empty, barren, ineffectual speculation, for the deviations of the professors of it, which probably stirred Ezra in my text. (such a scandal is not to be expiated with tears of blood). As the Duke of Urbins' painter being blamed for painting St. Peter and St. Paul too high colored, since fasting, mortification, labors, and watchings had discolored and paled their cheeks, wittily and tartly replied, *That those Apostles were one indeed while they lived, but they now blush to see those that pretend themselves to be successors, to succeed them no otherwise then as a disease doth heath, or night day.* All these reasons justify this blushing we speak of.

Application 1. *Conviction.* But O, how many degrees distant from this temper of Ezra's are those, who are so far from a modest resentment of others sins, that they never change color when they are convicted of their own! That can tear God's sacred name, dismember his Son between their teeth, out-face the sun, magistrate, minister in swinish drunkenness, goatish lust, savage oppressions, and what not, that would infect the air but to name? And yet are frontless. Like the contriver of the golden Legend; on whom a Papist could pass this verdict, that he had a laden heart, and a brazen face. We read of "a brow of brass" (Isa. 8:4); of a "whore's forehead" (Jer. 3:3); of "faces harder than rock" (Jer. 5:3); we have whole quarries of them; those impudent wretches died not without issue. Among all stations and ranks of persons that expostulation is not impertinent, "Were they not ashamed, when they had committed abominations? Nay, they were not ashamed, neither could they blush." (Jer. 8:12).

No, we are fallen on an age, into which those monsters have transmitted by a kind of transmigration, their spirits, contemporaries of St. Augustine, of whom he so complains, "Though nothing be blamable but sin, I, lest I should be blamed, was fain to be more sinful; I belied myself, that I was guilty of what I never committed, lest the more innocent I was, the more despicable I might appear." We are ashamed not to be shameless. At least, ashamed of what we should count our crown, religion, and profession. We are ashamed of our glory, and "glory in our shame," as heirs to those prostitutes that extorted tears from St. Paul's eyes but to name, (Phil.3:18-19). We have swarms of those that will with triumph, trumpet forth how many they have plundered, oppressed, ground to powder, ruined by their power; having no better plea then that of the wolf to the lamb, "Thou hast a better cause, but I have better teeth". boasting, how many unwary ones they have over-reached by flight of brain; with that hell-bred Proverb in their mouths, "Plain dealing is a jewel, but he that useth it shall die a beggar," (and yet it is a wonder, there should be so many beggars, and so few plain-dealing men), bragging how many pliant fouls, laden with sin, led away captive by lust they have ensnared, and subdued by their blandishments. Which impudence is to let out sin to use, to wind it up to the highest peg; and it is a link of the chain of sin fastened next to the gates of hell. And it is irrational, as if a felon should boast of his fetters, a dog of his vomit, an infected person of his plague-sore, or a possessed demoniac of his devil.

Dear Christians, if there is any shadow of ingenuity in us, I trust we shall rather take part with Ezra in the text, blushing for *other's* sins, than so insolently proclaim our own (like Sodom).

Exhortation 1. Let us not be ashamed of owning God. "I am not ashamed of the Gospel of Christ," (Paul says). (Rom. 1:16). No, he points to his chain, that he bore for Christ's cause, as children point where they are fine, (2 Tim. 1:16). The Celtes in Damascene thought it was a disgrace to withdraw themselves from a falling wall; let us be ashamed to flinch from God, though all the world should disclaim him. Our Lord

and Master will at the last day be ashamed of them that are
now ashamed of him, Mark 8:38. Let us not blush in a good
cause, where justice or mercy challenges our relief, though
justice or mercy should pass for a crime among men.

Exhortation 2. Let us blush rather for dishonorable,
dishonest, scurrilous, unworthy words, and actions. "Thou
shalt remember thy wages, and be ashamed, saith God to
Israel," (Ezek. 16:61).

Motive 1. What is past cannot be recalled; we cannot
be innocent, we may be penitent, though we cannot offer the
spotless lamb of "blamelessness"; we may the turtles of
"penitency," our two eyes filled with shame and sorrow. We
are ashamed of bodily defects, of asymmetry, disproportion of
parts; of which we are not guilty. We are guilty of our
spiritual deformity. As God argues to Moses about his sister
Miriam, "If her father had spit in her face, should she not have
been ashamed seven days?", and now she is a leper, let her be
shut out seven days, (Num. 12:14). So it holds by rules of
equivalence; if we be ashamed of what we are merely passive
in from our heavenly Father; why not much more for our sin,
wherein we have been culpably active?

Even nature (Tertullian says) has cast a shame-
fastness on all sinful evil. Malefactors refuse to appear. "They
that are drunk, are drunk *in the night*." It was so in St. Paul's
time, 1 Thess. 5:7. They tremble, and blush when apprehended;
deny, when accused; when tortured, they seldom, or hardly
confess; condemned, they bemoan themselves; and impute all,
either to the malevolent aspect of conjunction of stars; or to
the unresistableness of fate; they will not have guilt lie at their
door, because it is guilt, and opprobrious. Let but nature
work, it will prompt us to this modesty.

But grace, I hope, will be more expressive on us. "I have seen Ephraim (*God says*) smiting on his thigh;" I have heard his moaning, and acknowledging himself ashamed. It was melody in God's ears, that confession; and that smiting was a lovely prospect in his eye, as appears by God's melting, passionate language about him in the next verse. "Ephraim is my dear son, my pleasant child, I remember his still; my bowels are troubled for him; I will surely have mercy on him," (Jer. 31:-20). And when the soul-wounded Publican did not dare look up to heaven, instead, heaven looked down to him; he declined his own eyes, and inclined God's.

In a word. It was a strange thing (Augustine says) if in our faces there should be such a distance between our forehead and tongue, that "shame" should not suppress and stifle a "bold tongue". If Diodorus the Logician fell down dead for shame, that he could not resolve an argument propounded to him. I think if we were truly apprehensive of the multitude and horridness of our sins, and the venom naturally interwoven with our souls, and our unkind abuse of so gracious a God *we should blush even to death*. We would be ready to creep into the grave, or hell itself. We, having too much cause to take Ezra's words out of his mouth, and to appropriate them to ourselves, "For our iniquities are increased over our head, *etc.*"

I am fallen from the impression of his shame, to the expression of his and Israel's misery, (set down also as the ground of his shame). And that first in his self-arrangement and indictment filed against himself and Israel. In which bill, his ingenious confession comes first to hand; displaying their sins under the varied terms of iniquities and trespasses.

Iniquity in our English idiom sounds like injustice, and inequality. Indeed what is more unjust than sin? Especially the sin of those within the bosom of the Church who are favored and ennobled with so many mercies and privileges? "Are not my ways equal? and are not your ways unequal?" (Ezek. 18:25). We see God here expostulating with his people.

Trespasses is the other title Ezra gives their sins; which imports breaking bounds, and due limits, and invading another's right.

Another piece of the character of sin is that it leaps all hedges and ditches, breaks through all fences of relations or duties; and spares nor God, nor man.

But the Hebrew words run higher. The roots where they are borrowed, imply crookedness, perverseness, ignominious baseness to be exploded and hissed at; as the meanly versed in that tongue know.

The Jews were a crooked and perverse generation, as Steven stigmatizes them with it; offending against the clearest Revelation, and most remarkable dispensations of Divine providence, (Acts 7:51).

The truth is, all sin is crookedness, being a deflection from a straight rule. But there is more crookedness and perverseness in some sins and sinners, then in others.

For perverseness, we are generally like children, that because they cannot have what they will, throw away what they have, slight what they may have. And will endure a world of hardship and redoubled blows, rather than bend a knee, or give a word. There is a steely obstinacy, a twisted contrariety in our nature. Abraham's children turned to stones, to thwart John the Baptist that speaks of stones turned to children, (Matthew 3:9).

And crookedness, we so affect winding meanders, and turning labyrinths in our ways, that it may be said to us, as it was in the epilogue to the Serpent; that having his death wound, stretched out himself straight, (Isa. 59:8). You should have lived so; you have led a crooked life, and now you would die right and straight, and go straight to Heaven, like Balaam in his wish. But as the tree falls, so it lies; if death leaves it crooked, such will judgment find it.

But I spend but a word on words; and the variation of them; here Ezra goes on to aggravate Israel's sins.

The aggravation of them. From the dimensions of them first characterized in four or five expressions. 1. "Great," there is their continued quantity, their magnitude. 2. "Increased, multiplied," there is their discrete quantity, their multitude. 3. "Over our heads." 4. "Up to Heaven," there is their extension, as before their intention. And all these are of distinct consideration, for something may be great that does not multiply, and that may grow, which yet does not amount above our heads; and such may get above our heads, that yet does not ascend to heaven. Their sins were all like this.

1. "Great;" whether we eye that individual, particular sin, where Ezra took the hint of his lamentation; the people of God matching with idolatrous wives, which stole and ravished Solomon's heart from his God, so stupefying and infatuating him, that, like a bowling ball he began to slug toward the end of the alley, near his death, wracking even in the sight of the heaven, (1 Kings 11). A sin which Paul calls *unequal yoking*, importing as a great inconsistency as between light and darkness, righteousness and unrighteousness, Christ and Belial, (1 Cor. 6:15-16).

Or whether we contemplate their sin in general, it was *great*.

All sin is great, being an offence of a great, an infinite God. But yet sins are of different magnitudes. It is a Stoical fancy that they are equal. No, the same sins are greater or smaller in several persons. If St. Peter had had St. Paul's malice, and St. Paul had had St. Peter's knowledge, they had both committed the sin against the Holy Spirit. I shall but touch on the ingredients that make up a great sin, because I have far to go, and not much time to spend.

Sins are accounted great in God's geometry that are committed against clear light. They are so heinous, that in comparison Christ accounts other sins none, (John 15:21). A servant may unwarily rush on his master in the dark; but to tread on his foot, and to look him in the face, is insufferable. Great knowledge greatens sins for knowledge is like the Unicorns' horn, that does well in a wise and good man's hand, but ill on a beast's head.

Sins also against eminent mercies are great. God had rather his mercy should be unknown then slightened (Augustine says). "Do you require God thus ye foolish people?" Moses says, Deut.32:6. To requite good for good is but humane; to requite evil for evil is *carnal*; to requite good for evil is God-like; but to requite evil for good is *diabolical*.

And sins masked with a coverture of holiness; as Israel's were. And they are thence denominated an hypocritical Nation in one place, (Ezek.33:31). Such sins are of scarlet dye. There is no sin to that of under a pretext of Religion; as David said of Goliath's sword wrapped up in the linen ephod, "there is none to that," (1 Sam.). Hypocrisy we call double iniquity; and therefore the punishment of the hypocrite in hell is made the exemplar of the torment of the greatest sinners, "they shall have their portion with unbelievers," (Luke 12:46).

We had need to solicit God then, that though this Jebusite sin will continue in our coasts, our breasts, that yet he would guard us from sins, that lay waste the conscience. "Keep thy servant (prays David) from presumptuous sins, so shall I be innocent from the great transgression," (Psal.19;13). It is now a great commendation to a man, if it may be said of him (as Tacitus speaks) that he is without crying vices, though not within virtue; and he that doth the least mischief, is a Saint. But I cannot insist.

The second expression is, that sins were not only great, but *became still greater*; they were increased and multiplied, both in magnitude and multitude. as it is charged on them, that they revolted more and more, (Isa. 1:4).

First for continued quantity; sin will greaten, and wax, and grow, like drops to a torrent, a slip to a wood, a spark to a flame. The measure fills the space. We read of the fullness of the Amorites' sins. In good we are as conscionable as children; we do not care how little we have for our money; we give God gold hard weight; a *little* religion on a knives' point serves our turns; but we never set a period to the bulk of sin. "Lust (St. James says) having conceived, brings forth sin," and so proceeds to finishing, (Jam. 1:14-15). Sin has its *conception*, that is *delight*; and the *formation*, that is *design*; and the *birth*, that is the *acting*; and *custom* is the *education* of this brat; then follows a *reprobate sense*, and the next step is *Hell*. None declines to the worst at first, but gradually step by step; as mariners setting sail first lose sight of the shore, then of the houses, then of the steeples, then of mountains, and land. And as those that are waylaid by a consumption, first lose vigor, and then stomach, and then color.

Then the discrete quantity must not be omitted. "Our iniquities are increased and multiplied," So the Hebrew gives it. multiplied even above arithmetic; as sparks out of the oven's mouth.

Sins you see never go alone, but like the waves of the Sea, the end of the one is the beginning of another. David is a sad instance, he drew iniquity with cast-ropes, as Isaiah phrases it. First he is idle, then he lusts after another's wife, then he sends for her, then violates her chastity; when Uriah had but one Lamb in his bosom, and he had too many already. then he makes her Husband drunk, then plots his death, making the man contributory to his own death by bearing letters to Joab, and draws Joab also within the compass of the guilt, (Isa.5:28).

What need have we to attend that caution, "Take heed ye be not hardened by the deceitfulness of sin?" (Heb.3:13). We know where we begin and set out in a sin; but we know not where we shall end and take up. As no man can say he will let in so many pale-fulls of sea and no more. Many set up the trade of sweating with the common interlocutory oaths, as faith; many began thieving with pins and penny; many drunkenness with one cup more than enough; many lust with a glance of the eye; and never dreamed they should ever be prohibited to those prodigious extremities they after find themselves almost irrecoverably engulfed in. As when Pompey could not prevail with a city to billet his army with them, he yet persuaded them to admit of a few weak maimed soldiers, but those recovered their strength, and opened the gates to the whole army. The devil courts us only to lodge a sin of infirmity, or two, and they gathering strength, and sinews, subdue us. It will be our wisdom to nip sin in the bloom, the bud, right at the first and from mere suggestion; to kill this cockatrice in the egg. For if we go with sin one mile, it will compel us to go with it two. It will swell like the cloud Elijah saw, from the bigness of a man's hand to such an expansion that it will cover the sky. like the waters of the Sanctuary, that may at first reach to the ankles, but in tract of time increase over our heads.

3. Which is the third expression, I will but name it. Sin will mount above our heads, if it be suffered to take its course (Psa. 38:4). Above our heads so as to usurp, and tyrannize over us, to depress us, to render us contemptible, and to lay our honor in the dust. So over our heads, as to keep us down, so that we cannot look after our God. So above our heads, as to dull our brains, and make dull our understandings. God calls Israel a sottish (*drunk*) people; so above our heads as to drown us in perdition, this is how the Apostle speaks if God does not step in to help us, (1 Tim.6:9).

Is it not better to keep it down, then that sin should keep us under hatches, or our heads under water? O let us by faithful approaches to our Christ, drown our sins in the red sea of his blood; and in the waters of repentance, break the heads of these Dragons. Implore God for assistance, that sin may not get heart-high in our affection, or head-high in our thoughts and fancy, and much less gain such a supremacy as to climb over our heads.

4. A fourth expression remains, "Our trespass is grown up to the heaven". *To*, not *into* the heavens. Sin was bred there in the angels, but they were cast down from there, and shall never find their way back either. No unclean thing shall enter

there, (Rev. 21). If it could, it would darken the sun, put out the moon, seal up the constellations. But to the heavens, sin is so daring and bold to fly, whether to intercept the passage of our prayers there, or to stop the influence and the light of heaven from descending here; or to knock at heaven's gate to solicit for vengeance on us. The sin of Sodom we read had a "cry," and Abel's blood a cry; and Nineveh's sin came up afore God. And our sins often out-voice our prayers. (Gen. 18:20; Gen.4:10; John 1:6-9).

We have no remedy but to send our faith and prayers before them to heaven to prepossess our Savior, that he may be our Master of requests, our Advocate, Mediator, Intercessor, a screen between God's scorching wrath, and us. That he may plead for us both with words and wounds, for his blood speaks better things then the blood of Abel; the one calls for vindictive justice; the other for pardoning mercy, and obtains it; yes even for overgrown sins.

2. Which sin is an aggravation of Israel's iniquity, "From the days of our fathers have we been in a great sin unto this day." Sin is of a cleaving, adhering nature. It many times presses us to say with Augustine, O Lord, when was I ever innocent, there sin was. And it will not leave us if we welcome, and bed and board it. It hangs on to us (Paul says). It clings as swarthy blackness to the Ethiopian's skin, or spots to the leopard. It hides as leprosy to the house, that sometimes could not be scraped off; but the stones must be changed. No, sometimes the house is demolished. Sin, like the ivy on the wall, will not wholly be extirpated, until these earthen walls of ours be plucked down by death. Not soap, no nor fire and brimstone can wash off sin. It will not sound a retreat. No, when the body declines, sin gathers strength like the weary

ox, that takes the firmer footing. Messaline was wearied, but never satisfied with her baseness.

And that is the reason that the pains of hell are *eternal*, because we would sin *eternally*, would God lengthen out our lives here to eternity.

O! let us importune our God to cut the thread of our wickedness, that we may not spin it out to such a length. Let us every time break off this match, and sue out a divorce between us, and our darling sins. That God may never have occasion to say of us, as of Israel, Jer. 22:21. "This hath been thy manner from thy youth." *Break off thy sins*, Daniel says to Nebuchadnezzar, break this Gordian knot, (Dan.4:27).

It is not yet too late, the door of grace is still open, there is hope in Israel concerning this; as it follows. No, David has no better way for obtaining mercy then the greatness of the Lord who is merciful to his iniquity, for it is gross, (Ezra 10:2; Psa. 25:11).

Motive. The greater our sins are, the greater need we have of mercy. No man flies his counsel because his cause is great and intricate, but plies him the more. The more dangerous diseases are the more physicians are sought. Some offenders are like Darius' daughter, newly dead, by consent to some unjustifiable act; others, like the Widow's son of Nain, carrying out to burial, by acting unworthy things. Others, like Lazarus four days dead in the grave, stinking, and putrefying by living in sin, with the stone of custom rolled upon them. Let none of these despair; Christ can raise *all* these, as he did those. Do not defer true Reformation on this ground. *Man* is God's adverb, but the devils verb; God says work early, the devil says tarry. But though you have drawn out the line of sin to an undue length, do not cast away your confidence. Christ is good at an old sore, all cures are alike to him. Go to him by the paces of faith in the words of Ambrose, "O that thou wouldst be pleased to approach my monument, where my soul is enclosed; wouldst thou but weep over me, as thou didst over Lazarus, that he should live. That voice that commands thee to come forth, must enable thee, as him, to arise and walk his ways."

3. But Ezra calls us away to consider another aggravation of Israel's sin. It was epidemical, spreading universal, tainting all of all sorts, he includes himself, *he*; mentions here Kings, and Priests; but in the beginning of the chapter, prophets, people and rulers. He does not frigidly assert that they would all yield that uninformed; but he takes the boldness to lay the particularity of their offense, the height, greatness, multiplicity of sins at every one of their doors.

Observation. He that speaks promiscuously, and indistinctly to all, speaks to none. Reproofs and threats are often in Scripture styled burdens, and yet truly a burden is easily born away with a common shoulder. But when we "lay the axe to the root of the tree," and make our addresses from the pulpit, or otherwise, to special ranks of persons, and particularize their sins, when Nathan comes up close to David, with "Thou art the man;" this pricks the heart. And though a David may take it acceptably at our hands, yet most will kick and fling. Luther said knowingly, "To preach is nothing else but to derive peoples fury on our heads; to stir up a wasp's nest; to pull down an old house on us." How impatient were Stevens' hearers, Acts 7:34? And Paul's Acts 22:22? And in those glasses we may see our own temper. But what though? We must not betray our own souls, nor yours by our silence. If you could take order that the biting texts of Scripture had an expurgatory index passed on them from heaven; we poor spirited men are too prone to desire to sleep in a whole skin. But if we blot out these passages, we shall be blotted out of the book of life. And while they are standing here, a minister may be damned for his base silence. You will pardon us. Man may threaten prison, but God threatens hell. And truly a cock may have to leave to wake a lion. It is a pity great men should be let go quietly to hell more than the one which is meaner. He does not swallow his words, as if he had gone too far already in his indictment, but undauntedly goes on from an accusation to a condemnation of all Israel, rulers, and ruled; high, and low; supreme, and subordinate; rulers, priests, and people as accessory to their own misery. *For our iniquities have we, our Kings, and our Priests been delivered.*

2. Observe, that *self-accusation, and self-condemnation are two symptoms of a repentance that need not be repented of.*

Self-condemnation observed. They are marks ever to be found on cordial self-abasers; as we may collect from their language in Scripture, and elsewhere. Abram cries, "I am but dust and ashes that speak to thee," (Gen. 18:27). Dust minds us of mortality, ashes of fire; as if he had deserved one and the other. Jacob, "I am less than the least of all thy mercies," (Gen. 32:10). David, "So brutish was I, even as a beast before thee," (Psa. 73). John Baptist, "I am not worthy to unloose his shoe." The Centurion, "I am unworthy thou shouldst come under my roof. St. Peter, "Depart from me, O Lord, I am a sinful man." St. Paul, "The least of Saints, the greatest of sinners." Mr. John Hooper in our martyrology, "Lord, I am hell, thou art heaven. I a sink of sin, thou a fount of grace." John Bradford, "I am deaf as a stone, as dumb as a nail; a hard-hearted, a painted hypocrite, as he subscribes some of his Epistles. And so we find Ezra here; for he still involves himself.

Application. Let us mimic these copies. Every man has a Country Palatinate within his bosom; and may arraign and judge himself, and it is our security to do so. If we judged ourselves, we should not be judged, (1 Cor. 11:30). He shall by this save God a labor. Let us spare this man, who does not spare himself. He that justifies himself fights with God hand to hand, and is likely to lose. He that lies down at God's feet, reaches him his hand to lift him up again. "He that humbleth himself shall be exalted," (Luk.18:24).

But we must look a little nearer to these words, "From our iniquities have we been delivered."

There is a deliverance from evil, and to evil; the later is before us now. It is a delivery, a tradition, and resignation of us over to misery.

And the whole nation was passive in it. In this pronoun (*we*) are concluded all besides the Kings and Priests here specified. Each sort had peculiar sins for which they hurt; and all for all. "From the crown of the head to the soul of the feet there is no sound part," as Isaiah complains, (Isa. 1:5-6).

Observation. Sometimes a nation's sickness begins at the head, the Rulers. as the Shunamites' child complained of his head. Sometimes at the feet, the inferiors; as Asa's disease was in his feet. Sometimes the upper and lower parts of the body politic mutually contribute to each other's' ruin; as we read, that the sins of the people moved God to suffer Satan to tempt David to number the people, (1 Sam. 14:1-2); and then David's sin determined in a plague on his people by passion; on himself by compassion and sympathy, as the ice begets the water, and the water the ice. As in the natural body the stomach sends up vapors to the head, and the head sends down humors and distillations on the stomach and lungs. As the Sun inhales vapors from the earth, and returns them in thunder and tempests. As Noah was drunk with his own wine, Goliath beheaded by his own sword, the rose destroyed by the canker bred in itself, the beast by a self-bred wolf; the apple by the worm; the worms belly eaten through by the young vipers; Agrippina killed by Nero, to whom she gave breath, so are we undone by ourselves. Sin like a foolish friar whips itself. Punishment is connate, and innate to sin. "Fools because of their iniquities are afflicted," David says, Psa. 107:17-18. We may thank our own folly for our bane.

This point calls more for improving, then proof; from here forward therefore shall I apply myself.

I foresaw the time would prevent me; therefore I shall endeavor to continue the residue of my text in application, general and particular.

Application 1. General first. This observation, like a well-drawn picture, looks on all that look on it. It prompts us all, rulers, and ruled.

1. To justify our God in all his judiciary proceedings towards us. So did David, "That thou mayest be justified, and clear when thou judgest," (Psa. 51:4). So Daniel, "Righteousness belongs to thee. but to us confusion of face," (Dan. 9:7). The cup of the bitter waters of Marah, and Meribah, that we have drunk so deep of, is of our own mingling and embittering. The cuts and sores that have scourged us are of our own making. We have extorted thunderbolts out of God's hand; for he, like the bee, does not sting until provoked; or like the flint, on a collision with the

steel (our steely souls) he sends forth some hasty sparks. And *therefore,*

2. Patience well becomes us. It is unequal for the offender to murmur or repine at the offended, and justly incensed party. "I will bear (the Church says) the indignation of the Lord, because I have sinned against him." We have been long born with, and why should we not bear? Impatience, like the bulls struggling in the net, or the birds fluttering in the limetwigs, troubles, and fastens us, and engages us the more in affliction, whereas in patience we possess our souls (Christ says), By *faith* I possessed God; by *love*, my brothers; and by *patience* myself, (Luke 21:19).

3. Let God's vindictive justice be a restrictive to us from adventuring on any unwarrantable course; like a Cherubim with a flaming sword, to guard the way to any forbidden fruit, since it is like to cost us so dear, (Deut.29:19). Let us not be secure in our sins, nor bless ourselves in any way that God curses; God is merciful, but withal just; bountiful, but not lavish; he will spare till there be no remedy, as he did Israel, (2 Chron. 36:16); but though he has a lead foot, he has an iron hand, as it is said that Heruccius King of Algeir's had patience abused and converts to fury. When the snow of mercies melts, we are like to have a great flood. And as near as we are within prospect of peace and political happiness, we may miss of it; since I do not find that our sharp medicine has kindly wrought with us; lust, pride, excess, swearing, lying, deceit, gaming, voluptuousness, and others sins national (it were easy to be endless in naming but their kinds) ebb not at all, but flow; and a seat a Spring-tide. We are the more unsafe for being secure. When Adam was asleep he lost a rib; it is sad when irrecoverable ruin is the first sign of danger. Nor let us

bolster up ourselves with our spiritual church-privileges, as the ordinances or any other; they cannot exempt or shield us if we still provoke. There is no Sanctuary, no protection from presumption. As the Ark could not save Israel from the Philistines; nor the Temple the Jews from the Romans; nor the Palladium Troy from the Grecians; nor the Tombs of Martyrs Rome from the Goths, think not that God's quiver is spent; we read of an in-exhaust treasury of wrath, (Rom. 2:5).

My text instances in divers arrows feathered with wrath, and headed with ruin. Be pleased to cast your eyes on the text as I proceed.

What do you think of being delivered to men whose very mercies David calls cruelty? And therefore Nebuchadnezzar, I believe, sealed the den of lions in which Daniel was because he thought it was safer to trust him with the lions, that with him implacable enemies.

To be delivered to the sword, sad experience, the band of fools, has shown that it is better than I can decipher it. Joel calls the day of war (Joel 2) a day of gloomy and thick pitchy darkness. Elijah in 2 Kings 8:1 wept to think about it. The poison hemlock of hostility, Tertullian calls it. It is a stroke or plague like Pandora's box. It is a compound of plagues, a bar to religion. The temple went slowly on when they were accustomed to fight with one hand and to build with the other. It is said in 1 Kings 5:3. "David could not build God's house for the wars about him." It silences Laws, cuts the sinews, of traffic and trading, stifles arts and learning; though some birds of prey can fatten in hard weather, when all other fowls are pined. When you hear in the Trojan war that 870,000 Greeks and 670,000 Trojans were slain. 1,000,000 were slain in the civil wars of France, 10000 churches equaled with the ground. That in our Pharisaic field in the quarrels between the houses of the Turk and Lancaster fell 100,000. Can we find in our hearts to hug and harbor our old iniquities, and to do what lies to move God to spin this war we are currently in to all eternity?

To be delivered to captivity and bondage, to be salves (it may be) to slaves, God can reduce us to this. To be delivered to spoil, your houses, granaries emptied, see what all your labors over the years have gone to another, all the years of providence to be given to another. God can do this if we stay in our sin.

We could be delivered from our shame and confusion, to be a pity to our friends, a scorn to our foes; to be a by-word. Nothing pierces ingenuous spirits more than shame and scorn. The Apostle Paul thought mockings were cruel (Heb. 11:36). No word so sharp as the tongue. It flies lightly, but wounds deeply. To all these disasters can God expose us.

O do not let us continue to be cruel to ourselves, but for your own sakes (if you do not value God's honor) for the wives sake of your heart, for your children's sake which you pretend to tender as the apple of your eyes, the signet of your right hand, your heart-strings, lay what I have said to hear, if not, we can but weep in secret for you. To confess sin this day, and to persist in it, is to profess, This I have done, this I will do. To beat our breasts, and not to reform, is to harden them. But I must not forget my main errand hither.

You, Right Honorable, have summoned me to attend you in this fervor, and I know you would not have me prevaricate, or forfeit my truth. Give me leave to make my humble address to you in serious exhortation. My text specifies the guilt of King, and Priests, and people and as the third verse affirms. That the Princes and Rulers were chief in the trespass. I do not come here to upbraid, but with all humility to advise you to what you are newly concerned in, both in reference to yourselves and us, for the aversion of that wrath, that is gone out against us, and is to be read in legible characters on us; and for prevention (as much as in you lies) of that unundation of miseries, that it may be the heavens are big with, ready to be delivered, if your failings prove the mid-wives. Kings and Priests are in the text and rulers in the chapter. But Kings here are none, and I hope no priests, therefore I shall meddle neither with crowns nor miters. I do not love to speak to the absent, but the present rulers; here are a ring of auditors, and you the diamond. Let me mind you what Jewels are a gloss to your cornets.

1. Prudence, you are our heads, and the head is the throne of prudence. It is prudence to be able to discern, between people and things indifferent, between tenderness of conscience and obstinacy. We must discern between zeal and laziness. Doeg is called a liar, though he spoke the truth of David because he did not speak the truth in love (Psalm 110:3). We must be able to discern between the church and state, and how actions outside the church will shrivel up prayer for us in the church. You strength lies in your head, in discernment, like Samson's strength resided in his hair. You have need of your eyes in your head, that sit at the helm, and steer between so many rocks and sands. God was in love with Solomon's request, who wished nothing more and nothing else but wisdom to manage his affairs (1 Kings 3:9-11).

Secondly, another sparkling gem is justice, without prudence is just Jesuital craft. Job counted justice his robe and diadem (Job 29:14). Philip of Macedon displaced a magistrate because he colored his beard, he was jealous he might color a cause too (Plutarch, *Moral* 1:3). You must be as men of truth, with unwaivering integrity such as Jethro's justicers were.

1. It is justice to be accessible. That petitioners may come to you and not your doors guarded with your living, as Solomon's throne was with lifeless lions. As it was said to Augustus, he that dares approach you does not seem to know your greatness. He does not dare, and does not seem to know your goodness. God's presence chamber is always open.

2. It is justice to have two ears, one for defendants, as well as one of the plaintiff. For although it is true, if it is enough to deny, who will be guilty? It is as true if it is enough to accuse, and who shall be innocent? Cain was accused ninety times, and his integrity still brought him off.

3. It is justice to award the accusers the same punishment they intended the accused, in case they do not make their accusation good. The geese in the capitol of Rome were to be beaten if they cackled without cause, yet they once saved the Capitol by cackling. And the dog's legs were to be broken that barked when no danger approached. Such punishment (Cicero says) aspires in courts of judicature deserve. And then those setting dogs do not dare to come before your tribunals. Detracters are more bound to restitution than thieves by how much the name preponderates the estate, if at least there can be any recompense for defamation. There are three things that may not be dallied with, our faith, our eye and our reputation.

It is justice to proportion the punishment to the offender. He is a strange man of justice that knocks out a man's brains to kill a wasp on his forehead. As Pollio has cast his servant to the Lampries, for breaking a glass. As the grand

Seigior of the Turks ripped nine Eunuchs for one melon that was eaten without leave.

5. It is the life-blood of justice to expedite justice, and not to turn it into wormwood by unjust sentences, or into vinegar by delays. To suffer poor souls to lie longer languishing at hopes hospital, than needs.

6. It is justice to be impartial, and not respect persons but cause. Companieus complains, that many men's offices and lands were taken from them running away in the bartell between Lewis XI and the Burganidians, and given to those that ran nine miles further than they.

But this justice must be intermixed with mercy and moderation. Psalm 104:1, "My song shall be of mercy and judgment," David says. The robes of judgment are usually with red streaked with white, the one color of severity, the other of mercy. You are the fathers of your country (Patricians described among the Romans) we would lock on you with veneration not slavish terror. You must bear with us, and bear us in your arms by love, in your hearts by care, on your shoulders by patience. Reverence is ill purchased by terrifying. When you are gone, fear goes to, but love will remain. Fear converts to hatred but love to veneration, Plinius says. Some seem to be so angry with other vices as if they envied them. A debonair gentleness is a grace to you. It will be hard to pardon others in sin if you are in sin. You should be like Noah putting forth your hand to pluck out oppressed ones into the ark of your protection, when floods are abroad.

Jerome wished Parmmachius, a noble man, to be an eye to the blind, a hand to the weak, and a foot to the lame. Vespian would mourn over just punishments, and when he was to sign the death of any would say, "I would I could not a letter of the book." What difference between a man, and a brazen statue of a man, but that one is alive and one is not. Sylla was a devil to command Marcel Pletorius to be slain where he stood because he fell into a swoon at the sight of an execution. The first ever was revenged on virtue. It was a sad thing that the Jews were happy to purchase leave to weep. You resemble God whom you represent, no way nearer by mercy, the loveliest of his attributes, and should he take his advantage, we would all be lost men. You are never more like yourselves than when you are merciful. To lie prostrate to a lion saves the life. To be on the highest ground should be no advantage to a generous spirit; only cowards and ignoble are cruel. The ancient nobility of Rome and Arcadia wore moons on their shoes to remind them of the world's mutability. The highest may come to stand in need of mercy; with what hearts they can expect it, what face will you ask this that denied it? Judge merciless to them that show no mercy. Appius took away all appeals in cases of life and death, and when he came to need an appeal, he was justly denied it. Eutrepius endeavored to take away the relief of sanctuaries and himself was afterward hauled out of a sanctuary from the very horns of the altar. To show mercy, Chrysostom says, is a greater work than to build magnificent temples, no, to raise the dead.

Fourthly, shall I add love and incline ableness too, and studiousness of peace which adorns you. War (I trust) shall ever be your refuge, never your choice. To war as to marriage, not lust of gain, or dissention, but procreation of peace should be the motive. Carry peace in your hearts when the sword is in your hands. Hercules' club was made of the olive, the emblem of peace. It is a fit speech for a Spanish mouth that the smell of gunpowder in the field is as sweet as of incense at the altar. Love of bloodshed becomes the scarlet whore of Rome whose religion was planted in and watered with blood. Let the killing of twelve million in 42 years in the West Indies attested by Bartholomew a Casa (who was a Bishop there). Let French massacres, Sicilian even songs, Spanish inquisitions (which Heinsius aptly calls the *fourth fury*) let these things fill Popish chronicles and not furnish ours.

Fifthly, patience and temper render you honorable in men's eyes, passion exposes to contempt. None can rule well that cannot rule themselves, but are overruled by passion. He that cannot guide a boat in a river, is unfit to steer a ship in a storm. It would make the most furious spirit dispassionate to hear of the great cruelty of the emperor Theodosius, when he gave life to his passion, though otherwise he is by Ambrose and others, famed for a most temperate, merciful, religious prince. This is because a servant of his was slain in an uproar in Thessalonica. In a rage caused a massacre to pass on the city, in that in three hours seven thousand innocent people were butchered. You have a great need to set a strong guard on your passions.

Sixthly, humility, lowliness becomes the high as well as the low, your Savior condescended to wash Judas' feet. Those feet trudged up and down to betray him, and that soil off, which he contracted with those walks. Pride is no true greatness, but a swelling excrescence. Nobleness by humility is made more noble. It was Fermius' advice to Pammuchius, vouchsafe to sometimes enter the lowest cells of the meanest. The proud in ascending, descended. The humble in descending, ascend in the sight of God and all good men.

Seventhly, religion makes you like Jethro's magistrates who were those in fear to God, though you are "gods" before men. You are but men of God. Do not plead you are descent unless you answer the worth of your predecessors. Do not let such a description be only those that have gone before you. We had rather admire you than have you glitter with some type of borrowed riches. Jerome says nobles are constrained by a kind of necessity not to degenerate from the height of their ancestors. As those on the ship of justice and peace, have your eye on heaven when your hand is on the helm of the ship. Why should not great and good stand together in you? God is *Optimus Maximus*, the best and greatest. These two attributes God has made occur in men such as Joseph, Obadiah, Nehemiah, Mordeccai, David, the Lord's disciples, the eunuch, Flavanius, Deretheus, Terentius and others who have shown themselves to be good. Indeed, there is no true greatness disjoined from goodness. Every man is as he is in God's books. Tertullian said of Augustine, the name of piety was gracious to him than that of power. The holiest man is the noblest on earth, Clementus says. Bernard says, "God is no respecter of persons, yet I know not how goodness in the noble takes us most; perhaps because it is usually more lacking in them."

8. As you must be good, so do good and be devoted to the public's good. The one profits only yourselves, and other profits us all. Do not be selfish, and do not tread inwardly. Pompey, being on an expedition to Sicily looking for corn, when it grew scarce in Rome, and dissuaded by his friends, objecting to all the dangers of the voyage, answered them, "It is more unnecessary that I should go than live." A heavy piece of iron, like a good patriot, will leave its particulars relation to the load-stone. Falling, it expresses its homage to earth, the common center of heavenly bodies.

If your Lordships are invested with these qualifications and express them, it will never be said that the unjust are set over the Law, the impious over religion, ignorance over learning, or monsters over men. And it may be written over your house door, as over the court of justice in Zant, "This place hates wickedness, loves peace, punishes, guilt, preserves law, and right, and honors and increases the good."

I cannot select a better verse than the last one in my text. It offers to my hand, coming in as unforced, as honey dropping from the comb.

Consider what we have and what we would have; what we would enjoy, and what we expect and desire. We may echo Ezra's words here. For a little space comes grace which has been showed.

We have reason to celebrate (as well as) Ezra or Israel) the *grace* shown to us from the Lord our God. He has loved this kingdom, because he would love it; the ground of his love is in his immutable self, and not in us. As it is said of his love to Israel, "The Lord did set his love upon you, because he loved you," (Deut. 7:7-8).

And this grace could no more conceal itself than the sun. It has shown itself in so many rivers and streams, in so many mercies, that we (if any nation under heaven) may say we have comprehended (or rather been comprehended) "the breadth and length, and depth, and height of God's love." The philosophers tell us of three dimensions, but the Apostle has found four in God's mercy (Eph. 3:18).

And we have had a large share in this grace that Ezra memorizes in the text. I will walk on his grounds. In grace, mercy remembered amid the judgment; in allies remitting and relaxation of God's heavy hand. He has not let out all his wrath, but corrected us in judgment, weight and measure. His punishments fall on this side, his mercies go beyond our merits, as David sings in Psalm 103:10. He takes away a part that might have stripped us of everything as Anitus said of Alcibiadus in Plotarch. He sends a fever that might cast into everlasting burnings. He scourges with rods that might with scorpions. He begins that might make an end to us. He has afflicted us for three or four years now with a civil sword, that he might have delivered us to a seventy years Babylonish Captivity.

We have a share in refreshing mercy (Isaiah 6 to the end). No, we were all forfeited to his justice. He has laid no more on us then he has enabled us to bear and given us a door, a passage out, as St. Paul says in 1 Cor. 10:13.

We have a share in settling grace, giving us a nail in his holy place, his church. The Gospel has irradiated and shed his clear beams without setting or eclipse for above forty years on us. We have been like Goshen, we have dwelt in his tabernacle and holy hill, as it is promised, though we have neglected the conditions there specified in the Psalm (15:1ff). We have deserved to be un-nationed, un-churched by a bill of divorce from heaven, to be tumbled as a ball into a strange land as it is in Jeremiah 22:18. Israel complains, they had possessed the sanctuary but a little while. We cannot say so.

Ezra is grateful in the text for grace in a little space. What do we owe for so long a possession? God has also lightened our eyes by outward saviors, as Jonathans were by honey. And we as he have received our honey at the end of a road that we might more value it.

By favors of a higher alloy he has enlightened our eyes that had the shadow of death on them. Which was Oecolampadius' support (his name signifies a *lamp* or *light*) on his death-bed, who when his friends asked him whether the light of the candle troubled him being so bright, clapped his hands on his chest and said, "Here I have sufficient light, the light of God's countenenace."

In a word, to defraud your patience no longer, God has revived our hearts (as Ezra speaks in the close of my text) we are even raised from the grave of a difficult war. We are comforted with hopes that we shall not, like raised Lazarus, fall back into the same grave again. And this comfort, as the height of affliction is like mercy at the guillotine, or the executioner's block. Like welcome showers to the chopped ground or like the sunbeams after this flood, like a shadow against a scorching heat.

Man would never in this way have spared man. Therefore David call his kindness to the house of Saul (that deserved ill at his hands) the "kindness of God," (2 Sam. 9:3), and not of man. Comfort is here entitled reviving or re-enlightening in the Hebrew idiom. It is a kind of resurrection. But I must take my leave.

Let me borrow rhetoric from St. Paul, "I beseech thee," or conjure you (men, brethren, fathers) by all these mercies and pledges of God's love (Rom. 12:1), and such others as we do not know of (for it is with mercy as with a globe, its thought, the unknown part of the word is greater than what is discovered) I beseech you that here mercy may be as nails fastened by the matter of assemblies (as Solomon elegantly) to propound these duties to you in your hearts, heads and lives. Let God's justice tutor us to be just. Let God's moderation and forbearance make an impression of mercy on us toward each other. And let us not do this by reiterating and repeating the same sins, or be guilty of worse crimes. Nor do we want to exasperate God to judgment, which is called his strange work (Isa. 28:21, *cf.* Gen. 3:8). God tells us the father ran to meet the prodigal, where he waited until the cool of the day to meet with Adam and curse him. Like the sun bidding for tomorrow before we are up, that we may not move God to put his mercies into a suit against us, and recover them out of our hands. As God chooses to express himself by the prophet, "I will recover my wheel and my flax that I lent," (Hosea 2:9).

But if neither judgment, nor mercy, neither glad nor sad tidings, neither the dark nor the bright side of the cloud of providence is operative with us we must take notice. You put your ministers to a stand, and pose us, who with Moses and St. Paul would have our own names blotted out of the book of life, as soon as yours, if we could help you, but God's counsel shall stand. However, we by dealing freely with you, shall free our own souls from being guilty of your blood. And as the prophet encourages himself though once he thought to give over preaching, thinking he labored and expended his strength in vain. "Then I said, I have laboured in vain, I have spent my strength for nought, and in vain: yet surely my judgment is with the LORD, and my work with my God," (Isa. 49:4). I will close with a final scripture from Paul, "I speak as to wise men; judge ye what I say," (1 Cor. 10:15).

FINIS

www.ingramcontent.com/pod-product-compliance
Lightning Source LLC
Chambersburg PA
CBHW031958080426
42735CB00007B/437